In Pursuit of Us

LeRoy Dunn

In Pursuit Of Us

LeRoy Dunn

Published by LeRoy Dunn, 2023.

Copyright

Table of Contents

Psalm 1

Blessed is the man
who walks not in the counsel
of the wicked,
nor stands in the way of sinners,
nor sits in the seat of scoffers;
but his delight is in the law of the
Lord,
and on his law he meditates day
and night.
He is like a tree
planted by streams of water
that yields fruit in its season,
and its leaf does not wither.
In all that he does, he prospers.
The wicked are not so,
but are like chaff
that the wind drives away.
Therefore the wicked will not stand in
the judgement,
nor sinners in the congregation of the
righteous;
for the Lord knows the way of
the righteous,
but the way of the wicked will perish.

Psalm 1, here and Psalm 2 at the end of this book, are not designated to any author. Many scholars believe that David wrote Psalm 2 however, that is based on the wording, not on any historical documentation. All the Psalms are Divinely inspired. Looking at it from that perspective makes me imagine Yahweh speaking directly to us in both Psalm 1 and 2.

Jesus spoke of building a house with a solid foundation, of bearing good fruit. Jeremiah 17:8 explains a tree planted by water will bear fruit in a drought. John the Baptist said Jesus will separate the grain from the chaff.

People in the Ancient Near East were the same as we are today. We struggle against the Law of Yahweh so that we might pursue worldly pleasures. We call the Law of Yahweh bondage without realizing the true freedom and peace that it brings to our souls.

Glossary

Yahweh: The Hebrew name of our Father. Originally written as *YHWH*, most scholars believe it to mean, "He brings into existence whatever exists." The Latinized name was Jehovah. After the Babylonian Exile in the 6th century BC, Jewish people ceased using Yahweh for two reasons. First, as Judaism became universal, the more common Hebrew noun *Elohim*, meaning "God," tended to replace His name, Yahweh, to demonstrate the universal sovereignty of Israel's God over all the false gods that were being worshiped. Second, the divine name was increasingly regarded as too sacred to be uttered; in the synagogues, it was replaced with Adonai ("My Lord"), which was translated in the Greek Septuagint (the earliest translation of the Old Testament) as *Kyrios* ("Lord").

I personally like the Hebrew name, Yahweh, just because it's Hebrew. And if you seek to have a close personal relationship with someone, wouldn't you use their name to address them instead of their title? Just a thought.

Yeshua: The Hebrew name for our Lord and Savior, Jesus Christ. The name *Jesus* derives from the Greek way of expressing His name, which is pronounced "Yay-soos." So, we ended up with an English version of the Greek version of the Hebrew name for our Messiah.

Yeshua was not a Christian; He was not a follower of Christ because He was Christ Himself. He was also Jewish—the Jewish Messiah. *Christo* is the Greek word for *Messiah*. Jesus Christ really means "Yeshua the Messiah." Or in Hebrew, "Yeshua ha Mashiach".

It was no accident that His name was distributed to all the world in Greek because it was the common spoken language of the day.

If you are more comfortable calling Him Jesus, continue to do so. He knows His sheep, and His sheep know His voice.

When Yeshua the Messiah returns, there will be many tears—both in horror over what we have done and in joy over the One in whom we have believed and placed our hope.

BC, Before Christ: Many use the term BCE, meaning "before the common era," so as not to offend those who do not believe in Jesus. Sorry, but truth does not change. It is BC.

AD, Anno Domini: This term is Latin for "in the year of our Lord." Again, a different term is being used so as not to offend: Common Era, or CE. Truth is truth, and it does not change.

I have placed other definitions within the text; however, I felt that it was important for you to understand why I used these specific terms before you begin reading.

The secular world view, driven by Satan, has sought to change the truth of the Bible so that everybody is included and accepted. However, by doing so, they have alienated a large portion of people. These people feel that they are hated by and separated from Yahweh. This is not so! He wants *everyone* to believe in His son, come to Him, be washed clean, and be presented before Him as perfect.

Foreword

What I hope to accomplish with this study is to maybe help someone with what Jesus called us to do. Make disciples. There are a lot of questions about how to go about presenting Jesus to others and a real fear of getting it wrong. I know, I was there. I wanted so desperately to share the good news of Jesus, but was afraid of saying the wrong thing, or maybe starting an argument. So much so that I would remain silent, even when I felt the prompting to speak. I don't like being afraid, so I started studying. First I read the Bible, then purchased study bibles, then I sought apologists who had written books and purchased them. Finally I started searching the internet, YouTube, and speaking with other, more mature Christians whom I respected. Now I can't stop, nor do I want to. Information just keeps flowing in and I am much more prepared to speak. I also discovered that someone else's salvation is not my responsibility. It is between them, Yeshua, The Holy Spirit, and Yahweh. After I share, I have completed my Great Commission. I continue to discuss if the person is so inclined, or I move on if they are not. This is my journey to making disciples.

I am a sinner!

There is absolutely no human way that I can save myself by being good and becoming acceptable to God!

I can be saved only by accepting Jesus Christ as my Lord and Savior, acknowledging that He is the Son of Yahweh who came to us and lived a sinless life, and believing that He sacrificially died on the cross for my sins, was resurrected, and ascended to sit at the right hand of our Father, our Creator, our God, Yahweh. I am washed clean of my sins through the blood of Jesus and made fully acceptable to Yahweh.

All glory to the Father and to the Son, Yahweh and Yeshua. Amen.

Love. Pure, undiluted love. This is the description of our Father Yahweh, His Son Yeshua, and the Holy Spirit of God.

Because Yahweh is the perfect father, His love and guidance are to be treasured and honored in everything that we do.

His Law and his guidance are presented to us in the Old Testament through stories and lessons about what happened when people followed the Law and what happened when they ignored the Law. These stories and lessons are very much transferrable to modern times. People are still people. We just have more toys from which to choose from and with which to commit sin with, (see 2 Chronicles 17:1 – 20:34, which describes Jehoshaphat's reign as King of Judah).

The Bible is also the story of our Creators pursuit of His creation, *us*. It tells of His sending prophets to give warning and to plead for His creation to turn back to Him and be saved.

Yahweh's instructions and discipline are meant to bring us closer to Him. They are for our benefit, not His; for our eternal blessing, not His.

I am broken!

Sin was introduced in the Garden of Eden, where the fall of man occurred. It was also where the Messiah was first promised: **"And I will put enmity between you and the woman, and between your seed and her Seed; he shall bruise your head, and you shall bruise His heel" (Genesis 3:15, NKJV).** Satan and his demons will promise much, but they will only bring pain, suffering, and separation from our Father (they will "bruise your feet"). The Messiah will defeat Satan ("bruise his head") and bring eternal life with no pain or suffering for those who believe in Yeshua and accept Yahweh's forgiveness. This battle for our souls has been raging since the fall.

The most significant event in history is recorded in the Bible. It is the death and resurrection of Yeshua the Messiah. This story permeates the entire Bible. There are over 300 direct prophecies about Yeshua, and that is a conservative number. There are many more that allude to the Messiah. The creation account shows Yahwehs sovereignty over His creation. The fall shows us why we need a savior. The history of Israel shows two things: 1) the historical context of the coming of the Son of God incarnate, and 2) humanity's inability to save itself through works, thus, its need for a savior.

Yahweh has given us free will. He has given us the right to choose our eternal destinies. The options are know God or no God, an eternity with Him or an eternity without Him. He does not want a Heaven full of robotic worshipers. Yahweh could create that for Himself. Instead, He desires a Heaven full of people who want to be there with Him.

Yahweh is pure and holy. He can neither lie nor go back on His promises. It's not that He *will* not; He *cannot*. His Law does not change or waver with the winds of change that affect us. No human frailty can be attributed to our Creator as it can be to false gods. His promise of eternal bliss with Him, or eternal suffering without Him, is truth that does not change. Yahweh gives us the choice. If we enjoy the pain and suffering of this world and turn from Him, then our reward is eternal, isolated damnation. If we hope for His eternal kingdom, believe in Yeshua, and seek to follow His Law, our reward is eternal life with Him in Heaven.

Choosing to love and to follow the worlds system is denying the work performed on the cross by Jesus for us. It is denying the existence of the Law and therefore denying the work of the Holy Spirit, Jesus Christ, and our Father Yahweh.

Yahweh is pure, but I am not. Yahweh is righteous, but I am not. Yahweh cannot abide where there is sin. Therefore, He will not allow me into His presence unless I am washed clean of sin. He promises to *gift* me righteousness through my belief in Yeshua the Messiah. My unshakeable belief in Yeshua's death and resurrection is my narrow path to salvation. It is the only way to enter the Kingdom of Yahweh.

He asks us to have faith—in His promises, in Yeshua, and in the Holy Spirit.

The Oxford Dictionary defines courage as "the ability to do something that frightens one." Courage is not the absence of fear; it is the ability to move forward in spite of fear. In the military, we trained extensively for high-stress situations so that when we came under fire—and fear became a very real and present thing—muscle memory would take over and enable us to do our jobs.

The Oxford Dictionary defines faith as "complete trust or confidence in someone or something." Faith—in our Father and His promises, in Jesus and what He did for us on the cross, in the Holy Spirit's daily guidance—is what gives us the courage to face each day in a broken world.

Faith must be built through study of Scripture and prayer for wisdom and understanding. Through continued practice, faith becomes part of our muscle memory that takes over when courage is needed. It affords us the strength we need to do the job of spreading the word of the Gospel: "Then the eleven disciples went to Galilee, to the mountain where Jesus had told them to go. When they saw Him, they worshiped Him; but some doubted. Then Jesus came to them and said, *'All authority in heaven and on earth has been given to me. Therefore go and make disciples of all nations, baptizing them in the name of the Father and of the Son and of the Holy Spirit, and teaching them to obey everything I have commanded you. And surely I am with you always, to the very end of the age'* (Matthew 28:16-20, NIV).

Faith is not an insurance policy that keeps pain and suffering away, but it is a firm foundation that enables us to endure pain and suffering. Insurance does not stop the accident; it pays for the damage. Jesus is our life insurance.

I will repeat myself many times throughout this study. This is because I believe that each part of the message of the Bible is tied together through the theme of love and forgiveness offered by Yahweh.

Evangelism, making disciples, sharing the gospel, however you wish to define it, is an understanding of what Jesus taught before His accension, and the teachings in the Old Testament. To be effective at sharing the word requires a knowledge of oneself and an understanding of who you are speaking to. What set of presuppositions (things assumed beforehand) are you dealing with before you speak. Are they new believers, set in their ways through organized religion, or are they non-believers. All present a different set of challenges. In Acts 17, Paul introduces the One True God to the Athenians, who worshipped many gods and even had an altar to the unknown god. Paul used this 'unknown god' to make known the One True God. Meet them where they are and use love and understanding to speak and to help. If you do not know the answer immediately, do not give up. Admit that you wish to give the correct answer, research it, and share it. Apparently, you needed help also. We are all growing and maturing in our faith. This has happened to me a few times and I have come to welcome it because it increases my understanding while I am helping someone else.

I used many resources while writing this study, referencing and cross referencing so that I would grow in my understanding and faith. Through prayer, study, and many pauses to climb down from my soapbox, I hope to convey to you the love that I have found in the Holy Word of Yahweh through the Holy Spirit.

Websites:

gotquestions.org

bibleref.com

biblegateway.com

Expedition Bible by Joel P. Kramer on YouTube

Answers in Genesis and Is Genesis History?

Bibles:

MacArthur Study Bible, NKJV

Dr. David Jeremiah Study Bible, NKJV

Zondervan Study Bibles, ESV and NIV

Apologetics Study Bible, CSB

Books:

The Jesus I Never Knew by Philip Yancey

Person of Interest by J. Warner Wallace

Cold-Case Christianity by J. Warner Wallace

The Case for Christ by Lee Strobel

We are not to present the Word to others out of hate or judgment. We are *all* sinners in need of salvation. Narrow is the path that leads to the Kingdom of Heaven. ***"I am the way, the truth, and the life. No one comes to the Father except through Me"*** (John 14:6, NKJV).

My personal journey through this study has caused me to pause and take a closer look at myself. At times, it was scary and painful. Being honest with yourself and with Yahweh can elicit those emotions. It caused me to repent (feel remorse), turn away from my sin, and ask forgiveness, which was ***given!***

My sinful nature is still there, but I am aware of it. He is helping me to overcome it. I slip, I stumble, I fall flat. With faith, I know that Jesus is helping me stand up and dust myself off as I move forward anew.

All are offered this salvation, regardless of our pasts, our presents, our choices regarding sex, lies, or drugs. Jesus died for *us*! We are broken, all of us!

Only Yahweh is holy (*exclusive*).

Yahweh forgives everyone (*inclusive*).

The Ten Commandments

The Ten Commandments is a list of precepts, or laws, given to Moses on Mt. Sinai and engraved in stone around 1445 to 1446 BC. An Egyptian inscription from this time tells of YHWH's nomads wandering through the desert (YouTube, Expedition Bible, The Oldest Yahweh Inscription).

The nation of Israel was given these Laws to obey and honor. They were to show the surrounding nations the true nature of Yahweh and His blessings. The nation of Israel was not a powerful, conquering group of people. They were a small group of people that had just come out of 400 years of slavery. They had no organized military, no modern weapons of war, no lavish belongings, no home base to operate from. In our modern way of thinking, they were a group of ragtag, homeless vagabonds who could not strike terror in any established civilization. Yet, they had something that nobody else had. They had the One True God supporting them. Yahweh is who Canaan feared. Israel was the smallest and weakest of all the nations that surrounded them. Yahweh used this fact to show that He was sovereign, that He was in control. He gave Israel The Law to follow with clear instructions as to what would happen if they did not. Sometimes they obeyed, and Israel could not be defeated and prospered. Sometimes they did not obey, and the surrounding people attacked. Everyone knew that Yahweh was the one true God; some just chose to follow their carnal hearts (for example, the story of Jehoshaphat and his dealings with the northern tribes of Israel mentioned earlier).

The Jewish people have been persecuted from the very beginning. Not because of who they are, but because of who they represent. Yahweh. The persecution of Israel increased after the world realized that the Savior of mankind, was Jewish. Yeshua came "first to the Jew, then to the Gentile." Romans 1:16.

The secular worldview of the Ten Commandments is based on the idea that the people of the Ancient Near East knew them, and the Nation of Israel adopted them as their own. This implies that everyone followed them, but such was not the case. Everybody throughout history has known Yahwehs moral laws, even today. (Romans 1:19-23) This belief is like taking one sentence from an entire novel and using it to form a theory that is acceptable to the masses. You need to read the entire thing to see the whole truth.

Yes, *everyone* knew Yahweh and His Law, (e.g., the sailors and Ninevites in the book of Jonah), but many had chosen demons, idols, and carnality over Him. They convinced themselves that if it felt good, it was okay. Those in charge wanted selfishness, lies, and murder. They wanted power over the people. Sounds eerily familiar, doesn't it?

From Adam to Noah, all knew the one true God, but most chose not to follow Him: "The Lord saw how great the wickedness of the human race had become on the earth, and that every inclination of the thoughts of the human heart was only evil all the time" (Genesis 6:5, NIV). Thoughts of people's hearts were evil to the core, and they were destroyed.

From Noah to Abraham, all knew Yahweh, but most chose pagan or demon worship to satisfy their carnal instincts. Some chose to follow the one true God. For example, Melchizedek (Genesis 14:18-20, Hebrews 7:3) was a king and priest of Salem (Jerusalem) during the time of Abraham. Melchizedek foreshadowed who Jesus is to us: our King and High Priest. Scripture's mention of him tells us that even in the time of Abraham, before Israel was formed, some worshiped the one true God.

Expedition Bible's YouTube channel documents the archeological studies of Jericho. These studies verified that the biblical history is true. Then, the country of Jordan took control of the site and hired an atheist to lead a new study. She dated the site much earlier than the biblical account and claimed to disprove the biblical history. However, she based her theory on the absence of a particular style of pottery that was not found. Only *copies* of the pottery were found, so she said that history could not have unfolded as the Bible claims. ***But copies can only be made of something that exists***. You can't make this stuff up. She really said that, and non-believers eat it up.

Theory cannot replace truth.

There is another secular theory that the entire Bible was written all at once after the first century. Wrong again. Expedition Bible also shows two silver scrolls that contain a portion from Numbers dating back to the first temple period (the time of King Solomon, 970 to 931 BC).

There is much archeological evidence in support of the Bible's people and events. The mainstream secular worldview chooses to ignore or change the narrative to satisfy the desires of the masses.

Truth does not change to fit the desires of the world; the world changes to fit the desires of truth—every time.

Abraham was declared righteous for his *faith* in the promises of the Lord. Through his seed (Jesus), all nations would be saved. The Law was introduced 430 years after Abraham. The Law shows how to walk with the Lord. It also shows how we fall short and proves that we cannot be justified by following the Law only. We simply cannot do it! Faith in the Lord's promises came first, and it is still the only way. Faith is "being sure of what we hope for and certain of what we do not see" (Hebrews 11:1, NIV).

Each of the laws we are about to study was spoken with love and about love. They show that no human can perfectly obey the Law and that sins must be atoned for. A Savior was promised, but in the meantime, sacrifices of perfect first fruits, (e.g., animals, grain) were offered for the atonement of sin. The Savior's sacrifice would atone for all who believe. Yeshua was Yahweh's perfect first fruit given for us. Both made the ultimate sacrifice for us. No greater love exists than this. Yahweh and Yeshua did more for us through their sacrifices than He has asked us to do for Him.

Yahweh sent many prophets to call His people back to Him so that He could keep them safe and therefore show other nations His true self. Yahwehs love for His creation knows no bounds. He also sent prophets to other nations besides Israel, Jonah for example, whose message from Yahweh saved Nineveh. Yahweh used Daniel to bring King Nebuchadnezzar of Babylonia to belief in the One True God along with the Magi who visited Jesus at His birth.

Many of these prophets were executed for their words just as the Apostles and early Christians were executed for the truth. Yet, under threat of persecution and death, they still spoke the truth. None of them were perfect people. They were followers of Yahweh and Yeshua. Our God uses imperfect people to deliver His message of love, grace, and salvation.

Yahwehs' pursuit of *all* His creation has never wavered or lessened. It is happening now. Pastors in the pulpit speak of saving grace, many authors have written the proofs of Yahweh and Jesus, the scientific discoveries that were first read about in the Bible, and the prophecies about the future that we are seeing come true today, all point us to our Creator and to our Savior.

The Ten Commandments show us the character of Yahweh and show us just how far we fall short of righteousness.

The following study is using the New King James Version.

"And God spoke all these words, saying: 'I am the Lord your God, who brought you out of the land of Egypt, out of the house of bondage. You shall have no other gods before Me. You shall not make for yourself a carved image–any likeness of anything that is in heaven above, or that is in the earth beneath, or that is in the water under the earth; you shall not bow down to them nor serve them. For I the Lord your God, am a jealous God, visiting the iniquity of the fathers upon the children to the third and fourth generations of those who hate Me, but showing mercy to thousands, to those who love Me and keep My commandments'" (Exodus 20:1-6).

Oh my! Have we ever messed this one up!

Any object, pastime, person, or daydream that we put before Yahweh is an idol.

Vehicles, articles of clothing, houses, and electronics are just a few of the objects available to us that we prioritize more than our Creator.

Hobbies or leisure activities that take priority over our relationships with God have become idols.

If we feel that it is more important to see a game, concert, or movie than it is to spend time with our Father, then we are worshipping an idol. Famous actors and athletes even carry the title of "idol" with pride. This is not good for several reasons.

It is not wrong to have nice things or go to games, concerts, and movies. These things are fine. It is the importance we place on them that matters. Yahweh sees and feels what we place first in our hearts. I cannot imagine the amount of pain that I have caused my Father in Heaven by prioritizing other things above Him, but I know that He is anxiously and patiently waiting to forgive me.

My thoughts and actions reveal the contents of my heart, and He sees my heart.

Worshiping man-made idols can make us feel like we are in control, but attempting to take control is an unhealthy choice. It always has been and always will be. Humanity has been messing things up since the beginning. Yahweh tries to show us that, by placing Him and His Law first, life will be better than we can imagine.

Yahweh loves us (His creation) more than we can fathom. His love is greater than anything we have ever encountered in this world of greed, self-indulgence, and self-worship. Instant gratification is a drug that we never stop trying to find, and we are willing to hurt others to obtain it. How can that be presented as *good*?

Yahweh warns us that there is evil in the world, and we are to steer clear of it. Demons, or fallen angels, are powerful and evil. They lure us through our carnal desires. In his book *Return of the Gods*, Jonathan Cahn (a Messianic Jewish Rabbi and founder of Beth Israel Worship Center in Wayne, New Jersey) details who the demons are and what they promote. We turn to these false gods because they claim that greed, sexual immorality, and sacrifice of innocent lives for personal gain are acceptable. In a world where these false gods are worshiped, hate and distrust are commonplace. This is not what Yahweh intended for us. He set guidelines for us to follow that will keep us safe within His embrace. Unfortunately, we who were created in His image are not doing very well.

We are to love Yahweh above all. The pain caused to our Father when we do not love Him is immense and deep.

Many say that they believe in God and are therefore okay. Hmmm...even Satan and his demons believe in God (James 2:19). Think on that for a moment.

"You shall not take the name of the Lord your God in vain, for the Lord will not hold him guiltless who takes His name in vain" (Exodus 20:7).

"But let your 'Yes' be 'Yes' and your 'No,' 'No.' For whatever is more than these is from the evil one" (Matthew 5:37).

When I say "yes" or "no," I should say them truthfully.

Do not use His name to legitimize your words. If you use the name of our Father to strengthen your words, but your words are not true, or you do not keep the promise, then you are essentially saying that you do not believe in Yahweh. Or, if you do profess to believe, then you are saying that He is insignificant in comparison to your desires. This conveys to others that Yahweh is not real or that He is small. I do not think this falls under the Great Commission.

Just be honest. If your answer is "no," then say "no." If it is "yes," then say "yes." Keep it simple. A few moments of discomfort after telling someone "no" far outweighs the days, weeks, or even years of discomfort caused by a "yes" that should have been no.

Read Matthew 5:33-37. We are to spread the Gospel and live our lives according to it. If we do not follow every Law set forth by Yahweh, we are not sharing the truth found in the Bible.

By making Him unbelievable, we are once again causing Yahweh deep hurt.

"Remember the Sabbath Day, to keep it holy. Six days you shall labor and do all your work, but the seventh is the Sabbath of the Lord your God. In it you shall do no work: you, nor your son, nor your daughter, nor your male servant, nor your female servant, nor your cattle, nor your stranger who is within your gates. For in six days the Lord made the heavens and the earth, the sea, and all that is in them, and rested the seventh day. Therefore the Lord blessed the Sabbath day and hallowed it" (Exodus 20:8-11).

The Sabbath was given as a day of rest, a day for the Israelites to remember all that Yahweh had done and provided for them. Israel was to remember and to worship the Creator on the Sabbath. It is a day to refresh us and renew our strength for the coming week. The word *sabbath* means rest.

When Jesus started His ministry, there were 1,521 commands that had been added to the Law by the Jewish leaders, (or organized religion today), commands that were not set forth by Yahweh. In doing so, the leaders made the Sabbath day a burden instead of the blessing that Yahweh intended it to be.

The Jewish Sabbath is on Saturday, and Sunday, the Lord's Day, is the first day of the week (Acts 20:7). Early Christians moved the day of worship to Sunday so as to honor the day of our Savior's resurrection.

The actions of a non-believing world have caused Sunday to be treated the same as any other day of the week, and we have allowed it to happen. The idea of staying home to watch a game instead of going to worship is worldwide. I am just as guilty of this as anybody else. I have been working on it.

Gathering to worship Yahweh and hearing the Word strengthens and refreshes us. Being with others as we learn and grow in faith builds our characters and opens our hearts to the guidance of the Holy Spirit.

Sometimes our schedules prevent us from going to Sunday worship. However, we can all choose to take one day every week to rest, worship, and learn. This discipline leads to more. It leads to Him being the first thing you think of every day and the last thing you think of every night. It is *awesome*!

If Sunday services are not accessible for you, there are other options to get involved, including small groups or Bible studies that meet during the week, mid-week church services, online groups, etc. The possibilities are available; we just need to reach out and get involved.

Ideally, we would live in a world in which Sunday worship would be easy (I am old enough to remember Blue Laws). Unfortunately, though, we do not, so it's up to us to choose a day.

In 1 Corinthians 16:2, the Apostle Paul tells the Corinthian believers, "On the first day of every week, each one of you should set aside a sum of money in keeping with your income" (NIV). I take this as guidance to establish Christian worship on Sunday, the first day of the week.

In Romans 14:5, Paul teaches, "One person considers one day more sacred than another; another considers every day alike. Each of them should be fully convinced in their own mind" (NIV). Whether you worship on one day or all seven days, *be fully committed*, but do not judge someone else because he doesn't do it your way. We should honor one another's choices about how we choose to worship as long as we follow the laws set forth by Yahweh. Worship and rest on whichever day of the week is available to you. There's no excuse if you must work on Sunday.

Wow, it's almost like Yahweh knew what would happen in the future. Imagine that!

As Christians, we should gather together for worship and fellowship. We should individually praise and give thanks to Yahweh every day. We should also serve others. Every day, give thanks to Jesus for what He accomplished on the cross. Without Jesus, we are lost.

Out of His love for us, Yahweh wants us to keep our focus on Him, and He will keep us safe if we do.

"Honor your father and your mother, that your days may be long upon the land which the Lord your God is giving you" (Exodus 20:12).

Good social order begins in the home, not in schools or therapy sessions. Learning about the consequences of your actions happens in the home. Learning to get along with different personalities and the roles they play in our lives also happens in the home. Why would we fail to honor our parents for guiding us in social, vocational, and biblical teachings? The examples set by our parents teach us how to behave in the world.

I fully understand that some of us have less than stellar parents; however, even they have taught us how *not* to be, and for that we should be grateful. If our parents do wrong, we should not follow their example; instead, we should be thankful for the lessons learned from their follies. Forgiving our parents for their mistakes and sins against us is a must for our spiritual growth. Through belief in Jesus, *all* our sins are forgiven. How then can we hold back forgiveness?

In Mark 7:8-12 we read where the Pharisees had instituted giving the benefits that should have gone to the parents where instead 'corban' (an offering devoted for God). We do sort of the same thing today. As soon as possible we shuffle our parents off to rest homes and go visit them on holidays, feeling good about how wonderful are the children that were raised by such mediocre parents. Not exactly honorable actions on our part.

Obeying and honoring our earthly parents sets us up to obey and honor our Father in Heaven, which then leads to good social order and a peaceful, fulfilled life (not a life without trials, but one in which we walk with our Father).

Imagine the help we can give and the love we can show to others who are suffering as we have suffered by guiding them toward the only source of true comfort in this world: Yahweh.

We could point fingers at all the sin around us, but that would be judgmental. It takes a village to raise a child, but this is a concept that we have largely ignored and moved away from. Do your part. Lead by a biblical example. *Do not* stand on the street corner and shout damnation. Walk with our Father by treating all as you would want to be treated. Help others, volunteer in schools and hospitals, and get active in your community. Put our Father and our Savior first in your life.

We are each responsible for our own actions, no blame can be cast on our upbringing or our influences.

Jesus set the example for us by submitting to both His earthly parents and His Father in Heaven.

Love your parents, even if you disagree with them.

"You shall not murder" (Exodus 20:13).

Both Hebrew and Greek have different words for "murder" and for "put to death." There are also different nuances for deaths caused by accidents, neglect, or carelessness. Unjustified or premeditated death is covered by this commandment.

Many arguments have arisen over the Nation of Israel and the killing they did to form their country. A whole book could be dedicated to this subject alone; however, what follows is the shortened version of my interpretation. Side note: the Nation of Israel was not strong by themselves; they were outnumbered and outgunned, but they had Yahweh, and everyone knew it.

Ham, a son of Noah, had four sons; Cush (Ethiopians), Mizraim (Egyptians), Put (Libyans), and Canaan (Canaanites). These people *knew* who Yahweh was and what his laws were. They chose not to worship Him and instead worshiped demons and false gods that fed their carnal desires. Sexual immorality and child sacrifice were the norm in Canaanite society (YouTube, Expedition Bible, Excavated Canaanite High Place: "the sin of the Amorites"). In Genesis 15:16, the Lord tells Abraham that his descendants would **"return here, for the**

iniquity of the Amorites (in Canaan) **is not yet complete."** They had the opportunity to return to the one true God, but they chose not to. They were put to death, not murdered.

Courts used the early translation of the Bible as a guideline. In Romans 13:1-7, the Apostle Paul talks about the state's right to take the lives of evildoers (in other words, capital punishment). Life was hard during biblical times, and accidental deaths occurred. Refuge cities were designated for perpetrators of manslaughter (Exodus 21:13, Joshua 20). Also, Exodus 21:12-27 explains the Law concerning violence. Yahweh detests violence when it occurs because of anger, malice, or revenge.

We must also realize that Yahweh defines murder as any thought or feeling of deep-seated hatred or malice against another person. It includes not only the physical act of killing someone, but also the feelings that constitute murder. When we hate someone, we commit murder in our hearts and in the eyes of our God.

Forgive quickly and earnestly because feelings lead to actions.

Biologyonline.com defines *life* as "a characteristic of a living organism that distinguishes the latter from a dead organism or a non-living thing, as specifically distinguished by the **capacity** to grow, metabolize, respond (to stimuli), adapt, and reproduce."

Let that sink in for a moment. The **CAPACITY** to grow, metabolize, etc. is all that is required for life! Even the worshiped discipline of science says that life begins at fertilization. Abortion is murder. A medical procedure to save a life is not an abortion; it is a medical procedure. We cannot let "save a life" be defined as "my plans for my life are over," nor can we support abortion as a means of birth control. Sexual immorality is a sin for a reason. Dictionaries also use this same definition of life.

"When Elizabeth heard Mary's greeting, the baby leaped inside her, and Elizabeth was filled with the Holy Spirit" (Luke 1:41, CSB).

This happened just a short time after conception.

"For it was you who created my inward parts; you knit me together in my mother's womb. I will praise you because I have been remarkably and wondrously made" (Psalm 139:13-14, CSB).

King David knew the definition of life when he wrote this psalm around 1010 BC. Science knows the definition today. Changing the definition does not change the truth.

Abortion has affected me and many others. The Population Reference Bureau reports that there are 73,000,000 abortions worldwide every year (prb.org/resources/abortion-a-global-overview/). Personally, I have experienced the deaths of two children—one by a motor vehicle accident, and one by abortion. As King David said, "But now he is dead. Why should I fast? Can I bring him back again? I shall go to him, but he will not return to me" (2 Samuel 12:23, ESV). I know that my children await me, and I will see them again.

Forgiveness is freely offered and given, but repentance is demanded. So, ask for forgiveness.

Adoptions cost thousands of dollars and are difficult to carry out, yet abortions are cheap and easy. Why not flip that? If you want an abortion, get one; after all, it is your choice (it's still wrong, though). But pay for it yourself. Let tax dollars go towards adoption and help for unwed mothers. They feel scared and alone. We need to come alongside them and walk through this with them rather than ostracizing them or making them feel less than us. We ALL make mistakes, and God forgives us through Jesus Christ. It seems simple to me.

I suggest going to a used bookstore and finding a dictionary because definitions might change over time.

We are all created in the image of God, and all human life is sacred. Therefore, the unjust taking of a human life is forbidden. Yahweh gives us the Law as a guide.

We are to love our neighbors, and if we love someone, we will not purposefully cause them harm.

"You shall not commit adultery" (Exodus 20:14).

This commandment is intended to protect the sanctity of marriage between a man and a woman (see Genesis 2:24 and Matthew 19:5). Marriage was created by God as a sacred union between man and woman to complement and complete each other. Marriage is the foundation of a well-functioning society. It also mirrors the marriage of Jesus to the church. Yahweh designed marriage, so He defines it.

In the Bible, the only excuse for divorce is adultery (sexual immorality). Adultery stems from selfishness, self-worship, and callous disregard for your spouse's feelings. It causes a deep-seated pain that only those who have experienced it can fully understand.

Are you feeling unappreciated, ignored, or set aside? These are feelings that must be discussed within the marriage, not with outsiders (unless the couple seeks Christian marriage counseling). Telling a friend about your problems invariably leads to talking about them with someone of the opposite sex, and that easily leads to adultery, whether physically or in your heart. Regardless, it's the same sin.

Guard your marriage with intense fervor. Your partner is the only person in the world whom you both want to be mad at and wish to make up with. You have made a home together; you have made little people together. For goodness' sake, you have a dog and a goldfish together! *Work it out.*

The church is the bride of Jesus, and He will never let us down. That is the example we need to follow and the model that we need to reveal to the outside world.

The Nation of Israel did not develop out of nowhere. Yahweh established it, starting with Abraham and Sarah. As God's chosen people, they were to be a beacon for others to see the true blessings that come from the one true God. They were to reflect Yahweh's character in their everyday lives. His people were to be holy, for He is holy (Leviticus 11:44).

Jesus clarified that even sexually immoral thoughts are sins in the eyes of Yahweh.

So, how do we change ourselves? The short answer is that we cannot. Only our Savior can truly change our hearts. It does, however, take active participation on our part. We must want to change.

Accept Jesus Christ as your Lord and Savior and repent. Ask forgiveness, and it will be given by Yahweh. Study the Word of God and allow the Holy Spirit to guide you. Then practice what you learn.

Yahweh does not wish to condemn us; He wants ALL of us to have fellowship with Him. It is our job as believers to proclaim the good news of Jesus Christ, and it is up to each individual to accept or reject it. There are no hard feelings or condemnation from us because only God knows our hearts; no one else does. We are not to judge. We are to share, to love, and to stand. No matter what, we stand firm in the faith.

"Therefore put on the full armor of God, so that when the day of evil comes, you may be able to stand your ground, and after you have done everything, to stand" (Ephesians 6:13, NIV).

The Apostle Paul is awesome. Talk about someone who sinned, was forgiven, and then stood firm. Read about him if you wish to know about the Christian life.

Remember that Yahweh is love, and we are to show Him to others.

"You shall not steal" (Exodus 20:15).

Why would you want to steal from someone you love? That may sound like a strange question, but we do it all the time.

Theft comes in many forms. The obvious one involves taking a physical object that does not belong to us. The other forms are obvious but overlooked.

Taking an unauthorized break at work, leaving early, and arriving late are ways we steal from our employers. We should complete every task as though it were for God because, in the long run, it is.

Failing to spend time with your children or teaching them that sin is okay are forms of stealing from them because our job as parental units is to foster their development as healthy, functioning members of society.

Believe it or not, cheating on taxes is also a form of stealing. Jesus commanded us to give Caesar what is his. Whether we agree with it or not, tax codes are part of the law, and as Christians, we must follow the law. If we don't follow this law, how will we follow the Law of Yahweh? Of course, this does not apply to laws that go against the Law of Yahweh; those are to be fought against. Remember: *stand.*

Hoarding what God has given us for ourselves instead of using it to further the Kingdom of Heaven is stealing from Yahweh. Everything we have is a gift from Yahweh and truly belongs to Him. Our time and our money came from Him, and we should use them for Him. We can tithe with our time by volunteering at a homeless shelter, with widows and orphans, or at a retirement home. These are just a few examples. We can also tithe with our income—first to the local church, then to causes that further the Kingdom. Crisis pregnancy centers, single parents, and beggars on the street can all benefit from our generosity. We must steward our time and money wisely to support ourselves and others who are less fortunate or in trouble. In this way, we further the Kingdom of Yahweh.

Be honest, work hard, and give generously.

"You shall not bear false witness against your neighbor" (Exodus 20:16).

Why would we lie to or about someone we love?

Again, this may seem like a strange question, but we are called to love everyone. That's what "your neighbor" means. We are called to love everyone, whether we agree with them or not. We are not to support sin or allow it in our lives, but we are to speak and lead with love.

Satan is the father of lies. Many will succumb to the lie in the last days. Lies will be celebrated as if they are truth and the truth will be shunned, ridiculed, and persecuted. Many will proclaim themselves wise so that they may lead others to the shame of the lie.

On a person-to-person basis, bearing false witness (lying) about someone is equated to committing violence against them (Psalm 27:12) and is compared to a violent weapon (Proverbs 25:18).

There is no justification for telling a lie. Hollywood portrays it as a viable means to an end in many movies. Some feel that lies can be leveraged for the greater good. *We can see now how that is working out for us.* I think that bread lines are just around the corner. Lies cause pain and suffering to others regardless of the intended purpose. Primarily, lies come from an evil heart.

True justice cannot be served through false testimony. Even a white lie causes harm. Telling someone a lie to spare their feelings does not help them grow and improve, nor does it help your relationship with them because you will harbor ill feelings towards the other person. These feelings will fester and grow until they explode.

We can see here that God knows us better than we know ourselves. He created us, and He loves us. His Law is for our benefit, not our hindrance.

Be tactfully, honest and sincere.

"You shall not covet your neighbor's house; you shall not covet your neighbor's wife, nor his male servant, nor his female servant, nor his ox, nor his donkey, nor anything that is your neighbor's" (Exodus 20:17).

The definition of the Hebrew word for *covet* is "to lust after or long for with great desire." *Neighbor* includes everyone you encounter; in today's digital climate, that means everyone on a global scale.

We are to keep our hearts from desiring that which belongs to someone else, whether it be their lawn mower (ox), their car (donkey), or their spouse (see Exodus 20:14).

Coveting is the result of envy, which will root itself into our hearts and lead us to commit all manner of sins. An evil heart bears an evil soul. Just as in Noah's day, when mankind's "thoughts…[were] only evil" (Genesis 6:5), evil leads to destruction.

Sin begins in the heart (James 1:15). Lusting after another's possession involves the same heart posture as the action of taking it. Admiration is one thing; envy is another.

The root of envy is the love of self above all else, including Yahweh. Worshiping yourself and/or objects is idolatry.

Inside our hearts, envy can take the form of idol worship, disobedience, murder (wanting someone gone so you can get what's theirs), adultery, theft, and lying.

Read the story of David and Bathsheba in 2 Samuel 11 (see gotquestions.org for a helpful explanation in the article, "What is the story of David and Bathsheba?").

It is not wrong to have nice things, but it is wrong to prioritize them above God. We are all susceptible to the trap of envy. We waste time, energy, and money to pursue things and people in vain attempts to fulfill ourselves. We can fall victim to thinking that a fancy vehicle, a bigger house, the latest electronic gadget, or a more attractive spouse will fulfill or complete us. In truth, when we feel unhappy, we think that we need bigger, fancier things. Depression sets in when we fail to achieve happiness through the empty promises of false gods and idol worship. Therapists make a good living from people who have this attitude or take this approach to life.

Only Yahweh can fulfill us and make us content. When we follow the teaching and guidance of our Father in Heaven, we will find true purpose and fulfillment.

The rewards for a life spent worshipping our Father in Heaven are not found in the trinkets that rust and decay; they are found in eternal life in Heaven with our Father and our Savior.

Yahweh gives us the choice of whether or not to follow His Law. Nothing has ever been said to the contrary. However, if we wish to spend eternity in Heaven, in fellowship with Yahweh and Yeshua, then we must confess our sins, turn away from them, and believe the Gospel: Jesus died for our sins and through Him, we are washed clean, and forgiven by Yahweh. Then we <u>must choose to</u> follow the Law of God. We will still stumble, and by this we know that we are lost without Jesus Christ. We will either experience eternity with our Father or eternity without Him. There is no other option.

As Christians, we cannot judge how others choose because the choice is theirs to make. We can speak the truth in love, but then we must move on. We have enough to do with concentrating on our own sinful natures that we shouldn't spend our time judging others. Only Yahweh and Yeshua can see into others' hearts and judge them fairly.

If we claim to be pure because we obey, then we are telling a lie. Our nature causes us to sin; we are carnal. We sin with our thoughts too. A battle goes on inside of us every day. That is why we can only be saved by belief in Jesus. By admitting this and accepting the grace given by Yahweh, we can help others find Jesus. *That* is our purpose, *not* judgment.

I will say it again: Yahweh wants all to be saved and spend eternity with Him, but He *will not* force us into His offer of salvation. His Law is available to anyone who wishes for it.

The verses that follow the Ten Commandments are Yahweh's instructions on how to follow the Law. They are also a clear indication that we cannot follow the Law perfectly. We always fall short, He knows this, and it is the reason He sent His Son, to be the perfect sacrifice for our salvation.

The Beatitudes

Mathew 5:3-12,NKJV

*B*eatitude: a state of utmost bliss (Merriam-Webster)

The Greek word is *Makarios*, meaning "happy, fortunate, blessed."

Blessed: happy, fortunate, blissful (Merriam-Webster)

Throughout history, man has associated blessing with the acquisition of more material possessions. It is not wrong to have stuff, but if you're constantly searching for more, it will bring stress and strife into your life. Marriages and relationships suffer because of the search for material things in a futile attempt to increase fulfillment in life.

How much better would it be to live humbly and quietly help others with our abundance? Yahweh sees what is done in secret (Matthew 6:4), but man sees what is done in public.

The Beatitudes describe true faith.

"Blessed are the poor in spirit, for theirs is the kingdom of heaven" (Matthew 5:3).

"Poor in spirit" does not mean being sad when my favorite team loses, getting upset that I did not win the lottery, or becoming unhappy due to my station in life.

Instead, it means being acutely aware of my utter spiritual failure apart from our Father and our Savior. I humbly recognize that I am lost and hopeless without the Divine Grace that is freely offered to everyone through our **Lord** and **Savior, Jesus Christ.**

This phrase has great importance in the description of our salvation. When we are honest with ourselves about our corrupted human instincts, our carnal natures, and our evil thoughts, that _should_ make us feel _lowly_. We are poor in spirit because we cannot enter the Kingdom of Heaven by being popular, wearing fine clothes, or driving a fancy car. Nor can we enter by simply being nice. Only by admitting to being broken, believing in Jesus, and accepting Yahweh's grace can we be saved. "Poor in spirit" is the exact opposite of self-sufficiency that has been celebrated throughout history.

I cannot be saved without Jesus. He alone is my path to salvation.

"Blessed are those who mourn, for they shall be comforted" (Matthew 5:4).

This is not referring to the mourning over a lost loved one, but rather to the mourning over sin that is within and around us, the sins that are abhorrent to Yahweh but celebrated by man.

We _are_ comforted in our grief when we lose loved ones, but that is explained elsewhere.

When I grieve and mourn over my sin, agreeing with Yahweh about my true nature, then I can humbly ask for forgiveness and be comforted by the Holy Spirit. I am comforted because my sins are forgiven forever. When Jesus died on the cross, He was made a perfect sacrifice for my sins.

Honesty with myself and with Yahweh allows me to truly see my sin. This comes through studying Scripture, searching my heart, and being aware of my day-to-day activities. As I pray for wisdom, understanding, and help, I more easily see my true nature. Thankfully, we are shown our sins one at a time so that we can deal with them and not become overwhelmed. He truly is loving and caring towards us—much more than we deserve.

"Blessed are the meek, for they shall inherit the earth" (Matthew 5:5).

Meek: enduring injury with patience and without resentment (Merriam-Webster)

The word *meek* has been equated with *weak* for a very long time. However, nothing could be further from the truth.

Meekness involves being in complete control of yourself through the power of the Holy Spirit, praying for help, and submitting to the Holy Spirit's guidance in times of persecution. It prevents us from stooping to the persecutors' level and giving in to the urge for retaliation. It enables us to pray for the persecutors' salvation.

Moses was meek. "Now the man Moses was very meek, above all the men which were upon the face of the earth" (Numbers 12:3, KJV). Moses submitted himself to the will of Yahweh and faced Pharaoh. This was not exactly an act of cowardice!

Jesus was meek. On the night before His crucifixion, anticipating what He was about to endure, He prayed, ***"Father, if you are willing, take this cup from me; yet not my will, but yours be done"*** (Luke 22:42, NIV).

On the cross, Jesus was beaten, bloody, and in immense, unimaginable pain. He was ridiculed and rejected both by His tormentors and by the very people whom He came to save. Yet, Jesus prayed for them. ***"Father, forgive them, for they do not know what they do"*** (Luke 23:34, NKJV). Jesus is the standard for meekness and true courage in the face of persecution. With a word, Jesus could have called down legions of Angels. However, our opportunity for salvation hinged on His choice to do His Fathers will.

From a Christian standpoint, meekness is faith in Yahweh. He will win, and by standing with and for Him, so will we.

Meekness requires true courage, continual fighting against our human nature, and trust in our Father's plans and character.

"Blessed are those who hunger and thirst for righteousness, for they shall be filled" (Matthew 5:6).

Righteous: acting in accord with Divine or moral law (Merriam-Webster)

I cannot become righteous in the eyes of my Father in Heaven by my own actions. Only by accepting Jesus Christ as my Lord and Savior will I be washed clean of my sins and presented before Yahweh as perfect in His eyes.

To hunger and thirst for something is to continuously long for it, wish for it, pray for it—to want it above all else.

Being in this frame of mind all the time allows the Holy Spirit to work within us and grow our understanding of Scripture, Yahweh, and Yeshua. It allows us to display the true nature of the Father and the Son to those around us. to show love, compassion, empathy, and understanding to everyone; by doing so, we evangelize through our actions. Our actions will be conversation starters as others want to know why we are so happy in a world that is coming apart at the seams. Our answer? ***Jesus***.

I will give my life to Jesus. I will not condemn, and I will not judge. I will show love by coming alongside those who need encouragement and offering them Jesus.

The feeling that you get when doing something in secret for Yahweh is nothing short of euphoric. It is a feeling that stays with you forever. It far outweighs the instant gratification offered by Satan.

I will stumble. As I grow, I will stumble less, but I will still stumble. See it, own it, and ask for Jesus. Once I am forgiven, I am forgiven forever. I will not lose my salvation, but I must continue my pursuit of righteousness. I will continue to study Scripture and pray for guidance and wisdom. Recognition of my sins comes from the Holy Spirit. I will never get good enough to do it on my own, nor do I want that. *I want to feel the teaching!*

Accept Jesus Christ, seek the Father through His Word, and listen to the Holy Spirit. Do so with diligence and joy!

"Blessed are the merciful, for they shall obtain mercy" (Matthew 5:7).

Merciful: compassionate (Merriam-Webster)

Mercy: compassion shown to an offender or to one subject to one's power (Merriam-Webster)

This one is straightforward. Mercy involves giving a lighter sentence to an offender who is truly repentant or who deserves a harsher sentence due to the severity of their crime.

I deserve eternal punishment for the sins that I have committed against my God!

He is pure in thought and deed; I am not. My sins cause great pain to my Father in Heaven, yet He forgives me—not because of anything I have accomplished, but because of what *Jesus* accomplished *for* me on the cross. Because of the redemption that is offered through Christ and accepted by me, I am forgiven and accepted (Hebrews 8:7-12). In His graciousness, Yahweh shows me mercy!

"He has told you, O man, what is good; and what does the Lord require of you but to do justice, and to love kindness, and to walk humbly with your God" (Micah 6:8 ESV)?

"Be merciful, even as your Father is merciful. Judge not, and you will not be judged; condemn not, and you will not be condemned; forgive, and you will be forgiven" (Luke 6:36-37, ESV).

It seems to me like we are supposed to pay it forward. Since we have been forgiven, we are to forgive others. Sometimes forgiveness is hard to give but keep at it because it will come easier over time. Yahweh sees our hearts and knows when we truly desire to forgive. He will help us to forgive. Actions (and prayer) speak louder than words.

To walk humbly with our Father is to know that good *only* comes from Him. We are not good by ourselves. We can only be good because of Him. Goodness is a gift from Yahweh that brings us peace and fulfillment.

Forgive quickly and with a glad heart. It brings the peace for which we search.

"Blessed are the pure in heart, for they shall see God" (Matthew 5:8).

Pure: unmixed, spotless, stainless (Merriam-Webster)

The Greek word for *pure* is *katharos*, which means "clean, blameless, or unstained from guilt." It can also refer to that which is purified by fire or pruning. Malachi describes the Messiah as a "refiner's fire" (Malachi 3:2). John the Baptist said that Jesus would baptize with the Holy Spirit and fire (Matthew 3:11). Jesus said that believers were the branches, and He was the vine (John 15:1-17). Pruning the bad away in us produces good fruit.

The Greek word for *heart* is *kardeeah*, which refers to both the physical heart and the spiritual center of life. It is where our thoughts, desires, purpose, will, understanding, and character reside.

(These last two paragraphs came from my research at gotquestions.org. Search "pure in heart" on their website, and you'll find even more information.)

Jesus taught that obeying God's Law in action alone is not enough. I am to obey out of my true love for Yahweh and my neighbors. I am to obey out of the desires to please my Father in Heaven and to avoid bringing harm to my neighbors. I am to speak and live the truth—not out of superiority, but out of humility. I am no better than anybody else. I have been saved by the work of *Jesus Christ* and by the grace of *Yahweh*. I am to proclaim this fact in love, humility, and gratitude. We do not become pure by ourselves, but by our belief in Jesus we are made pure.

Some will not be happy with the truth we proclaim. **<u>Do not</u>** take this to mean that you are causing harm. It is not harmful to speak the truth, but the way we say it can cause harm. Humble yourself and love the person to whom you are speaking. The only difference between nonbelievers and myself is *Jesus*. How can a nonbeliever have any chance of knowing Jesus if we present Him with an attitude of superiority or hate? If we present Jesus in this manner, then it becomes our fault that they lose out on salvation (Romans 14:13, 1 Corinthians 8:9). If we present the message of our Lord and Savior humbly and lovingly, but they still do not believe, then it is on them. ***"If anyone will not welcome you or listen to your words, leave that home or town and shake the dust off your feet"*** (Matthew 10:14, NIV). Some will believe, some will not. It is, after all, their choice.

I need to slow down and ask Yahweh for guidance with every situation that I encounter throughout my day. I need to ask Jesus to be with me and to fill my heart. I need to spend time with my Father in Heaven every day, reading His Word, praying to Him, and showing my gratitude and joy for the forgiveness of my sins. I need to give thanks to the Father and the Son for their love every day.

My hope is in Yeshua, my Lord and Savior.

"Blessed are the peacemakers, for they shall be called sons of God" (Matthew 5:9).

Peacemaker is a compound word that means "to practice peace." Peacemaking is an action. It's not just being nice. It may be kind, but it is not passive. It demands that we *step into* conflict rather than avoid it. Peacemakers initiate reconciliation when they have been wronged and are quick to repent when they have wronged others.

We have been conditioned to avoid conflict, but peacemaking requires moving toward it.

There is no peace without healing, and healing is only made possible by tough conversations and work.

Arguments, cross words, and any wrongdoings—whether real or imagined—must be brought forth and dealt with immediately. Letting them linger for any amount of time only increases the pain and places distance between the two parties.

Peacemakers must be committed to the truth. Many people believe that truth is relative and determined by the individual. **<u>NO!</u>** Truth is "the body of real things, events, and facts" (Merriam-Webster). Truth does not change. It is immovable. Truth comes from the Word of God, the Bible. As professing believers, we must live and speak this truth. As stated earlier, truth does not change to fit the world, the world changes to fit truth.

Peace depends on truth, whether it agrees with you or not. Justice, functional government, reconciliation, accountability, trust, humility, and love all disappear in the absence of truth (just look around at the world today). We must be committed to seeking and speaking the truth.

Understanding each other does not mean accepting false truths, but it does open the door for conversation and mutual love. We must not go against God's Law just to achieve a compromised peace with others. This is not true peace. We must speak the truth with love, compassion, and humility. Peacemakers cannot control others' acceptance of the truth, but we do have the responsibility of speaking it.

"Blessed are those who are persecuted for righteousness' sake, for theirs is the kingdom of heaven" (Matthew 5:10).

Persecuted: harassed or punished in a manner designed to injure, grieve, or afflict; caused to suffer because of belief (Merriam-Webster)

I will stand firm in my convictions about the Father and the Son. Many verses in the Bible pertain to this: 1 Corinthians 15:58, 16:13; Ephesians 6:11, 13; and 1 Peter 5:9, to list a few.

For me, this is where the rubber meets the road. If I believe in the truth of Yahweh, Yeshua, and the Bible, then my persecution is a foregone conclusion. It will happen. For some Christians in the world, persecution is a daily occurrence. They wake up to the threats of injury, jail, and death every morning. Our prayers for them need to be continual and earnest, for our turn is coming.

Speaking the truth is not popular in today's world. Truth is watered down or removed altogether, both in the media and in the pulpit. As a Christian and follower of the Way, I am committed to speaking the truth—not in anger or hate, but with love and compassion. I cannot and will not try to force belief in Yahweh and Yeshua upon someone else, but neither will I allow others to force false teaching upon me. Hence, persecution is a foregone conclusion.

"Beloved, do not think it strange concerning the fiery trial which is to try you, as though a strange thing happened to you; but rejoice to the extent that you partake of Christ's suffering, that when His glory is revealed, you may also be glad with exceeding joy. If you are reproached for the name of Christ, blessed are you, for the Spirit of glory and of God rests upon you. On their part He is blasphemed, but on your part He is glorified" (1 Peter 4:12-14, NKJV).

"If the world hates you, keep in mind that it hated me first" (John 15:18, NIV).

The Apostle Paul said, "For to me, to live is Christ and to die is gain" (Philippians 1:21, NIV).

I cannot waver as I stand for God, no matter the cost. Everything that is happening in the world was prophesied about two thousand years ago. If everything else in the Bible has come true, do you not think that the prophecies about the future will also come true? He has not lied to us, not once! He is telling us the truth <u>now!</u>

To hate others because of their sin would be to hate myself because of mine. To accept their sin would be to accept mine. Either way, I lose. I accept the Word of God as truth. He alone can judge fairly, and He will.

"Blessed are you when they revile and persecute you, and say all kinds of evil against you falsely for My sake. Rejoice and be exceedingly glad, for great is your reward in heaven, for so they persecuted the prophets who were before you" (Matthew 5:11-12).

Persecution is not something to be desired or sought out, but it *is* something to be celebrated. If we are persecuted for Jesus, then we are on the right path: the narrow and hard way (Matthew 7:13-14). Persecution is to be endured with a joyful heart as we stand on the truth of the Father, the Son, and the Holy Spirit.

Christians will be lied about and hated for standing with Jesus. Imprisonments, beatings, and executions are to be expected. These things are happening around the world *right now*!

These actions against Christians come because of unbelievers' fear and their refusal to give up their sins. They do not know Jesus, so they fear Him. Those in charge do not wish to give up their power and prestige, so they instigate hatred against Jesus and His followers. Christians are to *introduce* the love and compassion of Jesus and the Father to unbelievers. That is our *Great Commission*!

Everyone knows Yahweh. **"I will put My law in their minds, and write it on their hearts; and I will be their God, and they shall be My people"** (Jeremiah 31:33, NKJV).

We know the truth, but not everyone accepts the truth because it does not allow us to chase our carnal desires. The truth is ingrained deep within us. Some want to change the truth, but that is *impossible* to do. Truth is *constant* and *immutable*. Persecution arises out of fear and anger.

Those who are persecuted for faithfully following Jesus will be *greatly* rewarded in Heaven, not on Earth.

The Sermon on the Mount

Matthew 5:13-7:29,NKJV

The Sermon on the Mount is a complete explanation of the Law and a direct assault on Pharisaic legalism. It can also be transferred to the organized religions around the world today that teach a secular worldview instead of a Biblical worldview. The people of Israel were living under a system that Yahweh never intended. He knew it would happen, but it was not part of His design. Religious leaders had added much to God's Law and made it increasingly more difficult to follow and obey. Therefore, an attitude arose that deemed compliance with the Law impossible—so why try? Many were going through the motions of religion without true faith or assurance of salvation. Much is the same today.

The Apostle Paul taught, "But now the righteousness of God has been manifested apart from the law, although the Law and the Prophets bear witness to it—the righteousness of God through faith in Jesus Christ for all who believe. For there is no distinction: for all have sinned and fall short of the glory of God, and are justified by his grace as a gift, through the redemption that is in Christ Jesus, whom God put forward as a propitiation by his blood, to be received by faith. This was to show God's righteousness, because in his divine forbearance he had passed over former sins. It was to show his righteousness at the present time, so that he might be just and the justifier of the one who has faith in Jesus.

"Then what becomes of our boasting? It is excluded. By what kind of law? By the law of works? No, but by the law of faith. For we hold that one is justified by faith apart from works of the law. Or is God the God of Jews only? Is he not the God of Gentiles also? Yes, of Gentiles also, since God is one—who will justify the circumcised by faith and the uncircumcised through faith. Do we then overthrow the law by this faith? By no means! On the contrary, we uphold the Law" (Romans 3:21-31, ESV).

Faith in the promise comes first, then comes obedience to Yahweh by upholding His Law out of love for God, our Savior, the Holy Spirit, and His creation.

Believers Are Salt and Light

"<u>You</u> are the salt of the earth; but if the salt loses its flavor, how shall it be seasoned? It is <u>then good for nothing</u> but to be thrown out and trampled underfoot by men" (Matthew 5:13).

This verse compares Christians to salt, a preservative and flavor enhancer. Christians should enhance and influence the world around them for the betterment of all, just as salt does to the food with which it comes into contact. The betterment of all means to lead people to Christ with the truth, not make them feel better about their sins. If salt is contaminated with other, lesser minerals, it loses its effectiveness and becomes useful only as a means to keep weeds from growing on a path. This illustration describes a Christian who is contaminated by worldly things.

"You are the light of the world. A city that is set on a hill cannot be hidden. Nor do they light a lamp and put it under a basket, but on a lampstand, and it gives light to all who are in the house. Let your light so shine before men, that they may see your good works and glorify your Father in Heaven" (Matthew 5:14-16).

I need to live my life in such a way that shows everyone I encounter that I am a Christian who follows the one true God and my Savior. In doing so, glory goes to my Father in Heaven, my Creator.

This does not mean that I should call the news station and have them film me giving five bucks to a beggar. If I did that, my reward would only be with man. This *does* mean that I should slip the beggar a hundred and hurry away. The beggar will be grateful and give the glory to Yahweh. In this case, my reward will be stored up in Heaven.

My life must reflect the Father and the Son so that those who are so inclined will ask questions of me, enabling me to present Jesus to them.

Christ Fulfills the Law

"Do not think that I came to destroy the Law or the Prophets. I did not come to destroy but to fulfill. For assuredly, I say to you, till heaven and earth pass away, one jot or one tittle will by no means pass from the law till all is fulfilled. Whoever therefore breaks one of the least of these commandments, and teaches men so, shall be called least in the kingdom of heaven; but whoever does and teaches them, he shall be called great in the kingdom of heaven. For I say to you, that unless your righteousness exceeds the righteousness of the scribes and Pharisees, you will by no means enter the kingdom of heaven" (Matthew 5:17-20).

Scribes: members of a learned class in ancient Israel who studied the Old Testament and served as copyists, editors, teachers, and jurists

Pharisees: members of a Jewish sect during the intertestamental period (the centuries between the last book of the Old Testament and the first book of the New Testament) who were noted for strict observance of the Law's rites and ceremonies and for insistence upon the validity of their own oral traditions concerning the Law.

Jot: the smallest Hebrew letter

Tittle: a tiny extension on a Hebrew letter

I NEED TO STUDY AND ACT ON THE WORD OF GOD!

Jesus did not come to change or remove the Law in any way. Instead, He came to clearly explain the Law so that we could understand it and recognize false teachings or false gods. Then, He was sacrificed for us so that we could be saved.

Jesus is the fulfillment of Old Testament prophecy. The New Testament contains the explanations and the teachings of Jesus.

Today, many political and religious leaders are adding to and taking away from the Word of God. This is why Jesus taught us to know the truth—so that we can discern false teaching. You know that little voice in your head that screams "NO!"? That is Him. Even before reading Scripture, we would hear "NO!" **"I will put My law in their minds and write it on their hearts"** (Jeremiah 31:33). This verse from Jeremiah was for the Nation of Israel, however as said earlier, all know Yahwehs' moral Law, and the evidences of Yahweh and Jesus are all around us in His creation.

"For whoever keeps the whole law but fails in one point has become guilty of all of it." (James 2:10 ESV). All people are exactly the same in the sense that we all, at one time or another, have wished to pick and choose what to believe and what not to believe so that we could feel comfortable in our sin. If we decide that truth is too uncomfortable, then we gravitate toward other idols that allow us to commit sin—and even encourage us to celebrate it. Those who choose this path are reverting to worship of the old gods. They are engaging in apostasy, turning away from the one true God.

Baal stands before the New York Stock Exchange, the bronze bull. Ishtar (Greek: Aphrodite, Roman: Venus) has celebrated sexual depravity. Molek is also going strong through the sacrifice of our children for financial gain through abortion and neglect. To teach these sins is to teach others to follow these false gods and demons. It's a little heavy, but...

There is only one true God, and He loves us. *All of us!* He is reaching for us! Believe in Jesus. Accept Him and be forgiven.

Murder Begins in the Heart

"You have heard that it was said to those of old, 'You shall not murder, and whoever murders will be in danger of the judgement.' But I say to you that whoever is angry with his brother without a cause shall be in danger of the judgement" (Matthew 5:21-22).

I must not have anger in my heart towards anyone.

This is difficult at times; however, with persistent prayer, anger will be replaced by forgiveness.

In these verses, Jesus was neither negating the Law nor adding to it. He was explaining the spirit of the Law. Refraining from murder is good, but by holding anger or hatred in my heart, I am just as guilty as if I had committed murder. Yahweh sees into my heart.

Righteous anger differs greatly from prideful anger.

Anger that produces God's purpose is righteous. An example is anger aimed towards those who abuse others. The abused will begin to feel anger through their healing process.

Prideful anger distorts God's purpose. This type of anger leads us to hate and harm others. Holding onto anger causes us to sink into depression, which is where sin lives and where Satan can take control of us.

I must seek God in every circumstance.

"And whoever says to his brother, 'Raca!' [a derogatory term meaning "empty-headed"] ***shall be in danger of the council. But whoever says, 'You fool!' shall be in danger of hell fire"*** (Matthew 5:21).

Verbal abuse stems from the same feelings: anger and hatred. These feelings can also lead to murder. The Law is referring to the feelings that come from our hearts.

Anger breeds hatred, verbal abuse, physical abuse, and murder. Whether I directly harm someone in these ways or just imagine using them against someone, they are equal sins in the eyes of Yahweh. Have you ever been mad enough at someone that thoughts of harming them come to your imagination? Most of have had these thoughts at one point or another in our life. Have you ever teased someone, or made fun of them? This is what Jesus was teaching about.

Causing harm to someone for personal satisfaction (revenge) involves placing *our* desires before those of Yahweh. HE ALONE WILL JUDGE FAIRLY!

Lying about someone causes pain and suffering, and you will not have true peace because *you* will know the truth.

"Therefore if you bring your gift to the altar, and there remember that your brother has something against you, leave your gift there before the altar, and go your way. First be reconciled to your brother, and then come and offer your gift. Agree with your adversary quickly, while you are on the way with him, lest your adversary deliver you to the judge, the judge hand you over to the officer, and you be thrown into prison. Assuredly, I say to you, you will by no means get out of there till you have paid the last penny" (Matthew 5:23-26).

The gift that we present at the altar now is our life and how we present it. We offer ourselves.

My relationships with others influence my relationship with Yahweh.

Whether I have committed the wrong or it has been committed against me, reconciliation is ultimately my responsibility to pursue.

Living in conflict with others will bring anger and hate into both my heart and theirs, leading to a sinful existence.

This *does not* mean to be reconciled to sin. Coming to any kind of agreement that accepts or perpetuates sin goes against the Law of God.

Loving your neighbor—even if they are sinful—*does not* mean treating their sin as acceptable. It means *loving your neighbor* as you wish to be loved. I wish for anyone to point out if I am living against the Law of Yahweh. Whether they return the love or not, <u>we must love them.</u>

Adultery in the Heart

"You have heard that it was said to those of old, 'You shall not commit adultery.' But I say to you that whoever looks at a woman to lust for her has already committed adultery with her in his heart" (Matthew 5:27-28).

Most humans, including myself, are guilty of this sin.

If we look at another person lustfully, and either one of us is married, then we have committed adultery in the heart. Taking a second look or staring and wondering what they would be like is committing adultery of the heart.

Love is *not* sex. Love is respect.

Simplicity sometimes requires an explanation. When we respect our spouses, we seek to honor them. We will grow together and reflect the image of our Father and our Lord and Savior. We will help our spouses to grow and become the people Yahweh intended them to be.

When we respect others, we do the same for them. We give them the opportunity to do the same in their marriages rather than leading them down sinful paths.

This shows respect for ourselves and our own spiritual growth.

This shows respect for the Law of God, which is for our benefit and for the *glory* of Yahweh.

Admiring beauty is different. Our Father created beauty for us to admire. See beauty for what it is—*just beautiful.* It is not an *object* to lust after.

Maintaining respect and love for each other builds our resistance to lust. I do not wish to bring harm to *anyone.* How much easier would it be to avoid harming others if I loved and respected everyone?

Love is the absence of fear. "There is no fear in love; but perfect love casts out fear. Because fear involves torment. But he who fears has not been made perfect in love." 1 John 4:18 NKJV

"If your right eye causes you to sin, pluck it out and cast it from you; for it is more profitable for you that one of your members perish, than for your whole body to be cast into hell. And if your right hand causes

you to sin, cut it off and cast it from you; for it is more profitable for you that one of your members perish, than for your whole body to be cast into hell" (Matthew 5:29-30).

My sin must be dealt with drastically. **Get serious about removing sin.** Jesus is not saying that mutilation is the only solution to sin because that alone will not remove sin from our hearts. He's saying that we need to place as much distance as possible between ourselves and our sins. If the internet is causing me to sin, I should remove my computer or phone; if I sin by gambling, then I should stay away from casinos, and so on. Remove from your life that which tempts you to sin.

That is just the first step. The second step is to dive into the Word of God for strength, guidance, love, and understanding. Reach out for help and support. There is help! Yahweh loves us and wants us to seek help from Him. It will be *given*!

My sin must be handled by drastic measures because of its deadly effects on my soul.

We are going a little past this verse to discuss sexual immorality and its biblical definition that has been addressed in the last few verses, just so that we do not get prideful or take a position of superiority.

Sexual immorality is any form of sex outside of the confines of marriage between one man and one woman. *Simple,* right?

This should keep us humble before God and before those to whom we evangelize. From the "back seat of my '60 Chevy" (thank you, Bob Seger) to homosexuality and everything else in between, it is all the same sin of sexual immorality. Most of us are guilty of this sin. Same sin, same guilt. One form of sexual immorality is not worse than another. *Now that is true equality.* If we commit one sin, we are guilty of all. This is why Jesus came to us. It is why He died for us. We cannot enter Heaven and be presented to Yahweh unless we are cleansed of our sins. Believe in Jesus and what He accomplished on the cross for us.

We are all floating on the same small, muddy pond in the same small, leaking boat, all searching for the correct rudder to guide us to the clear stream that will save us. **Jesus** is our rudder and our clear water of life. He is the *only* reason that we are acceptable to the Father.

"Flee from sexual immorality. Every other sin a person commits is outside the body, but the sexual immoral person sins against his own body. Or do you not know that your body is a temple of the Holy Spirit within you, whom you have from God? You are not your own, for you were bought with a price. So glorify God in your body" (1 Corinthians 6:18- 20, ESV).

Sexuality is a gift from Yahweh. He created it, and He defines it.

One of the arguments against biblical ethics of sexuality is that times have changed, so biblical standards no longer apply.

Yahweh gave sex to us as a gift for procreation and for pleasure (read The Song of Solomon). Every time we have sex with someone, we leave a little piece of ourselves with them that we can never recover. Only Jesus can restore us, which is why Yahwehs' Law is so important.

We believe that greed, murder, and theft are sins, and we have *no problem* understanding this fact. We cannot pick and choose our individual conceptions of truth.

Yahweh's character does not change with the world's views. His Law and truth are just as relevant today as when they were written. Remember the Egyptian inscription? His laws have been written in stone for a very long time.

Marriage Is Sacred and Binding

"Furthermore it has been said, 'Whoever divorces his wife, let him give her a certificate of divorce.' But I say to you that whoever divorces his wife for any reason except sexual immorality causes her to commit adultery; and whoever marries a woman who is divorced commits adultery" (Matthew 5:31-32).

The Pharisees in ancient Israel interpreted Deuteronomy 24:1-4 to mean that divorce was permissible if you were unhappy or somehow displeased with your spouse. All that you needed was a certificate, a simple piece of paper, to make your divorce legal in the eyes of man. *Not so in the eyes of our God.*

We do the same thing today. No-fault divorce makes it possible to trade in your spouse for a new one if he doesn't buy you the right house or she doesn't cook and clean to your satisfaction.

Marriage counselors ask, "What would make you happy?" Our culture promotes the idea that life is short, and you deserve to be happy.

Life *is* short, but what they omit is that eternity is forever. Our actions in this short life will impact our eternal destinies.

Jesus corrected the Pharisees' misinterpretation of the Law. Yahweh created marriage not only as a source of happiness, but also as a way to increase our holiness and build His Kingdom. He will only recognize divorce that results from adultery (sexual immorality). No other reason is considered—not even your spouse's non-belief. As mentioned earlier, you have a dog and a goldfish! *Work it out!*

It's possible to come out on the other side of adversity together, as one. Now just how *awesome* is that?

Marriage is an institution created by Yahweh, but it is continually under attack by Satan. The devil knows that he is going down and wants to cause as much pain and suffering and take as many of us with him as he can on his way down.

Both parties should seek biblical counseling. If divorce happens for any reason other than adultery, and one or both parties get remarried to someone else, they are committing adultery. Marrying someone who was divorced for a reason other than infidelity causes them to commit adultery.

We *do not* want to cause others to sin!

Moreover, if everyone followed the biblical ethics of marriage and sex, what would be the result? More divorce or less? More actively engaged dads or less? More suffering in the world or less? Would STDs, teen pregnancies, and abortions increase or decrease?

As we have moved further away from a Biblical worldview, we have greatly increased our suffering. However, many place blame on our Father for not letting us do as we please (see the book of Revelation). Most do not realize that the more we pull away from His love, the closer we come to the pain of Satan.

Selfishness reigns instead of selflessness.

Jesus Forbids Oaths

"Again you have heard that it was said to those of old, 'You shall not swear falsely, but shall perform the oaths to the Lord.' But I say to you, do not swear at all: neither by heaven, for it is God's throne; nor by the earth, for it is His footstool; nor by Jerusalem, for it is the city of the great King. Nor shall you swear by your head, because you cannot make one hair white or black. But let your 'Yes' be 'Yes,' and your 'No,' 'No.' For whatever is more than these is from the evil one" (Matthew 5:33-37).

I am to tell the truth and refrain from invoking the name of God or anything made by Him to strengthen my words.

That is the meaning of these verses in a nutshell.

Taking oaths is permissible, encouraged, and sometimes demanded in many civic situations today (e.g., in court, in marriage, in medical fields, in the church). However, the flippant use of oaths in day-to-day dealings is being forbidden here.

When I swear an oath by Yahweh or anything that He made (which is everything), I am demanding that He stand by my word. If I lie or do not keep the promise, then I lessen the presence of Yahweh. I portray Him as insignificant. I hurt Him.

Jesus is teaching that I should act as though I am under oath in all my dealings with others. My word is my bond. I will speak the truth in all that I do, regardless of the worldly consequences or what others are doing. I am to fear Yahweh and the eternal consequences more than I fear man.

Yahweh cannot lie. He is pure. As a Christian and follower of Jesus, I am to live my life so as to present Yahweh to everyone I encounter.

As a carnal human, I will sometimes fail. I must repent, ask forgiveness, and move forward. With love and respect, I must reconcile with those whom I have sinned against.

The Sermon on the Mount (How to serve)

Go the Second Mile

"You have heard that it was said, 'An eye for an eye and a tooth for a tooth.' But I tell you not to resist an evil person. But whoever slaps you on your right cheek, turn the other to him also. If anyone wants to sue you and take away your tunic, let him have your cloak also. And whoever compels you to go one mile, go with him two. Give to him who asks you, and from him who wants to borrow from you do not turn away" (Matthew 5:38-42).

"An eye for an eye" was a precedent that promoted justice by limiting a punishment to fit the crime. It was a guideline for judges in civil matters. It was *not* intended to give everyone license to get even with whoever had wronged them.

These laws were for the benefit of individuals and society at large. The further we have drifted from the Law of God, the further our society has spiraled downward. Funny how that works.

Jesus was telling us to be humble and seek peace with those who have wronged us. We are not to seek revenge.

In His grace, Yahweh does not seek revenge against people who have wronged Him. Instead, He invites us into a relationship with Him. When we know and accept His Son, Jesus Christ, He offers us forgiveness. Jesus is quietly and politely knocking on our doors. If we turn Him away, He will be back. He does not give up on us.

Because Yahweh helps us when we ask, we too should humbly help others who ask. Do not consider yourself to be superior to those less fortunate than you. Give generously and trust that Yahweh will provide. The beggar trusted in God when he asked *you* for help.

I'm not saying that we should become pacifists who do not resist Satan and his demons. James 4:7 and 1 Peter 5:9 tell us to resist Satan and the evil that he practices daily. It is not wrong to defend yourself or others against evil or to seek justice (Luke 22:36), but it is wrong to retaliate through revenge. We are to absorb and forgive personal affronts rather than seeking revenge or retaliation. Even in self-defense, we are to use no means unnecessary or over the top in subduing the offender.

In giving, we are to not be gullible or naïve (Matthew 10:16; 2 Thessalonians 3:10), but if someone is in legitimate need, then sacrificial and purposeful giving is the proper response.

I cannot stoop to the level of evil. My response needs to reflect Jesus, who reflects Yahweh. Lying and cheating only produce more evil. By doing evil, I will only bring about more pain and separation from God. I *cannot* judge or *condemn* those who commit evil deeds. I can only seek Jesus in every situation.

Only Yahweh and Yeshua can judge fairly. Only they can see into the hearts of men.

Love Your Enemies

"You have heard that it was said, 'You shall love your neighbor and hate your enemy.' But I say to you, love your enemies, bless those who curse you, do good to those who hate you, and pray for those who spitefully use you and persecute you, that you may be sons of your Father in heaven; for He makes His sun rise on the evil and the good, and sends rain on the just and the unjust. For if you love those who love you, what reward have you? Do not even the tax collectors do the same? And if you greet your brethren only, what do you do more than others? Do not even the tax collectors do so? Therefore you shall be perfect, just as your Father in heaven is perfect" (Matthew 5:43-48).

I will love and pray for all people, regardless of how they feel about me, our Father, or our Savior.

People live in deliberate defiance of the Law of Yahweh. Christians are persecuted for speaking the truth. Jesus was executed. After all of this, Yahweh loves His creation and wishes to forgive the sins they have committed. However, there is only one way to forgiveness, and it is Jesus.

In Leviticus 19:18, God told us to love our neighbor. The Pharisees added the "hate your enemy" part. Remember that *neighbor* means **everybody**. Yahweh made the sun, rain, gentle breezes, and beautiful things for everyone, not just for believers. His love knows no discrimination; it is offered to all of creation, both good *and* bad.

The teachings of Yahweh in the Old Testament were about how to be good, not evil.

The wrath that comes from God is just and right. The Canaanites were brutal. They practiced incest and child sacrifice. God gave their land over to Israel with instructions to annihilate all Canaanites, thus removing their evil. Their sin was complete. Only God's wrath can produce righteousness, not man's wrath.

Anyone can be forgiven and brought into the Kingdom of Yahweh. Bathsheba committed adultery with King David. Rahab was a harlot in Jericho and a Canaanite woman. Ruth was a Moabite woman. All were women who had faith in the one true God. They are all in the genealogy of Jesus Christ.

True believers in Yahweh and Yeshua will love everyone without accepting their sins. I do not need to accept someone's sin to be able to love and care for them.

Yahweh gives blessings to all. We need to recognize this and give praise and thanks to the one true God. Yahweh judges and loves, we only love.

I will love and pray for all my Father's creation.

Do Good to Please God

"Take heed that you do not do your charitable deeds before men, to be seen by them. Otherwise you have no reward from your Father in heaven. Therefore, when you do a charitable deed, do not sound a trumpet before you as the hypocrites do in the synagogues and in the streets, that they may have glory from men. Assuredly, I say to you, they have their reward. But when you do a charitable deed, do not let your left hand know what your right hand is doing, that your charitable deed may be in secret; and your Father who sees in secret will Himself reward you openly" (Matthew 6:1-4).

Giving should come from the heart. It should be done for the Father's glory, not my own.

Open displays of perceived generosity—that are done for the express purpose of bringing attention to myself and showing how wonderful I am—do not bring glory to Yahweh. My reward for this action is complete. It is here with man.

Giving in secret (or anonymously) adds to my rewards in Heaven.

We can give not only with our money, but also with our time. For example, you can volunteer at a church, school, or rest homes. You can open a door for someone, allow others to go first, and listen to your neighbor's problems. Spend your life humbled by the generosity of our Father and pay it forward. Our time and money are gifts from Yahweh that should be stewarded for His glory.

Not everyone has a lot of money, but we do have time. Give monetarily when you can, and then give of your time. Be sacrificial in your generosity. Give up your vacation to help someone, and do not tell anyone.

In this digital age that we live in, cash is used less and less. Sometimes, it's inevitable that people will see you doing something good when you use a credit card. Do not let this dissuade you from doing good. Yahweh sees our hearts and knows our intentions. But do not make it a big deal. Do it and then move on.

"Jesus sat down opposite the place where the offerings were put and watched the crowd putting their money into the temple treasury. Many rich people threw in large amounts. But a poor widow came and put in two very small copper coins, worth only a few cents.

Calling His disciples to Him, Jesus said, *'Truly I tell you, this poor widow has put more into the treasury than all the others. They all gave out of their wealth; but she, out of her poverty, put in everything-all she had to live on'"* (Mark 12:41-44, NIV).

Giving strengthens our hearts for God and motivates us to do more for His glory. It is *awesome*!

It is not wrong to share Christian books that we have read with others, to serve openly in church, or to do anything good in public. Yahweh sees our hearts, and our intentions cannot be hidden from our Father.

Here are some additional verses on giving:

"He who sows sparingly will also reap sparingly, and he who sows bountifully will also reap bountifully. So let each one give as he purposes in his heart, not grudgingly or of necessity; for God loves a cheerful giver" (2 Corinthians 9:6-7).

"It is more blessed to give than to receive" (Acts 20:35).

"God shall supply all your need according to His riches in glory by Christ Jesus" (Philippians 4:19).

"Give generously" (Deuteronomy 15:10, NIV).

"Every man shall give as he is able, according to the blessing of the Lord your God which he has given you" (Deuteronomy 16:17).

"For God so loved the world that He gave His only begotten Son, that whoever believes in Him should not perish but have everlasting life" (John 3:16).

Now let us look at John 3:16, which describes the ultimate gift from our Father and our Savior.

No other verse describes Yahweh's relationship with humanity more clearly than this one. It's straight and to the point.

As a loving creator of all, He sent His only Son to be offered as the perfect sacrifice for *our* salvation. Yeshua died to save *us*! Imagine the pain that Yahweh suffered as a loving parent for our sake.

Jesus knowingly and willingly submitted to God as He suffered on the cross for *us*. He bore the punishment for *our* sins. *He* was our sacrificial lamb. Having been made fully man, He felt the pain just as a man would. As the Son of God, He felt, for the first time in His existence, the absence of His Father's presence because Yahweh cannot abide where there is sin. ***"My God, My God, why have You forsaken Me"*** (Matthew 27:46)?

Another interpretation of this verse is that Yahweh did not turn from His Son, because Jesus was a perfect and acceptable sacrifice, the planned salvation for mankind. Jesus was quoting the beginning of Psalm 22, and anyone who knew the psalm could finish it and see that it was speaking of Yeshua the Messiah.

As a parent and grandparent, I hurt when my children or grandchildren suffer pain.

I cannot imagine the depth of pain that Yahweh suffered from sacrificing His Son, nor can I imagine the immense pain that Jesus felt. Not only did He experience physical pain, but He also experienced anguish from knowing the sins of Israel.

*All of this was done for **us** and **our** salvation. That is true sacrificial love.*

I will give generously and sacrificially of my time and money. I will pray for a giving heart.

The Model Prayer

"And when you pray, you shall not be like the hypocrites. For they love to pray standing in the synagogues and on the corners of the streets, that they may be seen by men. Assuredly, I say to you, they have their reward. But you, when you pray, go into your room, and when you have shut your door, pray to your Father who is in the secret place; and your Father who sees in secret will reward you openly. And when you pray, do not use vain repetitions as the heathen do. For they think that they will be heard for their many words" (Matthew 6:5-7).

Praying with other believers (e.g., praying corporately in church or praying for someone while with them) is good and encouraged. This speaks to my intimate relationship with God.

Praying loudly in public for the purpose of being seen by others is hypocrisy. In this case, I have my reward from man, and the prayer is not heard. It is not meant as a prayer anyway; it is meant to raise myself up in the eyes of man. It's a form of self-worship and idolatry.

Hypocrite is a Greek word meaning "a character who wears a mask." Hypocrites are actors who portray someone else. Yahweh does not hear or reward hypocrisy. He does, however, punish it.

My prayers are personal conversations with my Father, my Creator, my God. My prayers should be simple and direct, like those of a child. I should leave out the extra words and phrases and simply speak with respect and love. After all, He is my Father, and He loves *me.*

"Therefore do not be like them. For your Father knows the things you have need of before you ask Him" (Matthew 6:8).

The quantity or eloquence of my words do not matter. God knows what I need before I ask. I need to keep it simple and direct, so that *I* understand what I am asking or saying. Yahweh already knows.

"In this manner, therefore pray" (Matthew 6:9):

This is a model prayer that was taught by Jesus. It is not a word-for-word liturgy. Praying by rote, habitual repetition lessens the meaning to *us.*

"Our Father in heaven, hallowed be Your name" (Matthew 6:9-13).

Yahweh is my Father, my Creator. The relationship I seek above all others is with the perfect Father, who has all the answers for my life. The answers to my questions may not be what I, a broken man, desire. The answers may make me uncomfortable as He gradually reveals them to me, but His answers are always right. Yahweh and Yeshua guide and chastise with loving and caring hands.

My Father is in Heaven above, but I am here below. I will see Heaven someday. I know this because of my belief in Jesus Christ, my Lord and Savior. He is my advocate before my Father. He paid the price for my sins.

Yahweh's name is hallowed, holy, set apart. By recognizing Him as such, I am asking Him to act in my life in a way that visibly demonstrates His holiness and glory. I want my Father to guide me and teach me to reflect His love and care for others, for *everybody*!

I will give generously of myself and my resources.

I will listen attentively as a stranger tells me their story.

I will act not for my own glory, but for my Father's glory.

"Your kingdom come. Your will be done on earth as it is in Heaven" (Matthew 6:10).

I want God to rule. I want peace, comfort, fulfillment, and contentment, and I want them *forever*. I know that these desires cannot be fulfilled completely here. But they will be in the Kingdom of Yahweh. I can only *go* there because of my Lord and Savior, Jesus Christ. We are eternal beings, so only the eternal will satisfy us.

I should not pray for *my* version of blessing, *my* version of happiness, or the actualization of *my* plans.

I *should* pray that my *Father's* goals for me will be actualized, for the Holy Spirit to enter me and guide me every minute so that my life will display the glory of God.

This is the only way that my life will truly be blessed—probably not with money, but definitely with peace and contentment. If money does come to me, I am to use it for the glory of Yahweh, not for my glory.

I will pray for God's will to be done in my life and in the world. I will pray for His Kingdom to advance, not mine.

I will pray to focus on God's will, not mine.

I will pray for the arrival of God's Kingdom on earth, as it is in Heaven.

"Give us this day our daily bread" (Matthew 6:11).

I will pray that God will meet my daily needs and those of others—not our wants, but our needs. I will look to God, rather than the world around me, for provision.

All is made possible by Yahweh. Regardless of who hands it to us, God provided it.

My goal with this prayer is to be content with a simple life in which all my needs are met. I will be grateful to God for what I have, for it all comes from Him.

"And forgive us our debts, as we forgive our debtors" (Matthew 6:12).

I will pray for forgiveness of my sins and for God to empower me to forgive those who sin against me.

My sins are my debts to Yahweh. My struggle with sin has gotten easier with time and prayer—not because I am better, but because Yahweh is wonderful. My strength comes from Him. My sin will remain in me until Jesus Christ, my King, returns and makes everything right. Through faith in Jesus and by my Father's grace, my sins will be forgiven.

I must also forgive others for their sins against me. How can I be forgiven if I do not forgive others?

"And do not lead us into temptation,
But deliver us from the evil one.
For Yours is the kingdom and the power and the glory forever.
Amen" (Matthew 6:13).

Yahweh does not tempt me with sin; Satan does. I will face trials that will leave me vulnerable to Satan's attacks. As I pray, I ask for God to help me avoid falling victim to these attacks. I know that if I pray to Yahweh and ask for Jesus to walk with me, then the Holy Spirit will be with me, I will succeed, and God will be glorified.

I will grow spiritually. I will have confidence in Yahweh.

I am a broken and carnal human being. Victory over sin gives glory to God because I cannot succeed without Him.

"For if you forgive men their trespasses, your heavenly Father will also forgive you. But if you do not forgive men their trespasses, neither will your Father forgive your trespasses" (Matthew 6:14-15).

These verses emphasize the importance of Matthew 6:12.

When I accepted Jesus Christ as my Lord and Savior, I was forgiven of *all* my sins and justified before God. I received a complete acquittal from guilt and the penalty of sin that I so richly deserve. Salvation will never be taken away from me. However, I am still a weak human, and I will sin. I need to recognize my sin, own up to it, repent, and ask forgiveness daily (if not immediately). I need to forgive others for their sins against me.

I am not better than anybody else. *Anybody*! I must stay in a constant state of humility because of the grace and forgiveness given to me by Yahweh. He forgives me of *much*.

Compared to the hurt I have caused Him, the sins against me are minimal and should be forgiven with *joy*, not begrudgingly.

However, there is one sin that is unforgivable.

"Therefore I say to you, every sin and blasphemy will be forgiven men, but the blasphemy <u>against</u> the Spirit will not be forgiven men. Anyone who speaks a word against the Son of Man, it will be forgiven him; but whoever speaks against the Holy Spirit, it will not be forgiven him, either in this age or in the age to come" (Matthew 12:31-32).

Blasphemy is defiant irreverence, denying the existence of God and the Spirit's work in the world through Jesus. All else will be forgiven.

Fasting to Be Seen Only by God

"Moreover, when you fast, do not be like the hypocrites, with a sad countenance. For they disfigure their faces that they may appear to men to be fasting. Assuredly, I say to you, they have their reward. But you, when you fast, anoint your head and wash your face, so that you do not appear to men to be fasting, but to your Father who is in the secret place; and your Father who sees in secret will reward you openly" (Matthew 6:16-18).

For a long time, I did not understand how fasting connected with prayer and worship. Through the study of several resources (which I mentioned at the beginning of this book), I found what I hope to provide as a simple answer.

According to gotquestions.org, "The theology [the study of religious faith, practice, and experience] of fasting is a theology of priorities in which believers are given the opportunity to express themselves in an undivided and intensive devotion to the Lord and to the concerns of spiritual life. This devotion will be expressed by abstaining for a short while from such normal things as food and drink, so as to enjoy a time of uninterrupted communion with our Father. Our 'confidence to enter the Most Holy Place by the blood of Jesus' (Hebrews 10:19), whether fasting or not fasting, is one of the most delightful parts of that 'better thing' which is ours in Christ. Prayer or fasting should not be a burden or a duty, but rather a celebration of God's goodness and mercy to His children" ("What is the connection between prayer and fasting?").

We can see how this passage relates to the earlier ones about public displays of good deeds and prayer. Fasting—whether short-term, daily, or however else you choose to practice it—is a means of worship that puts God first. It allows my prayer and worship to be uninterrupted by distractions. It sets apart my personal time with God. Maybe get up an hour earlier every day and spend time with God before coffee and breakfast. Delaying coffee is what I have a hard time with!

Fasting in the sight of men will be ignored by God because it is for me, not for Him.

I want to store up rewards in Heaven, not here on earth. My Father in Heaven sees what I do in secret, and my reward will be with Him.

Lay Up Treasures in Heaven

"Do not lay up for yourselves treasures on earth, where moth and rust destroy and where thieves break in and steal; but lay up for yourselves treasures in heaven, where neither moth nor rust destroys and where thieves do not break in and steal. For where your treasure is, there your heart will be also" (Matthew 6:19-21).

I will not value the things of earth more than the things of Heaven.

I will face many temptations that will try to pull my attention away from my Father in Heaven. Satan continually dangles bait in front of me, tempting me to worship idols such as money, objects, and self instead of my God.

Having money is not a sin, but what I do with it can be sinful. When faced with the choice between buying expensive material possessions or living simply and giving generously to causes that further the Kingdom of Yahweh, my decisions will determine whether I am storing up treasures on earth or in Heaven.

Having possessions is also not necessarily sinful, but do I really need the most expensive one? For example, do I need a seventy-inch television, or is a forty-inch sufficient? Both serve the same purpose, but if I choose the forty-inch television, then I have money left over to help others buy a meal for their children.

Without careful prayer and thought, we can easily get caught in the trap of self-worship. Satan is always on the prowl, and we cannot resist him alone. We should slow down and think, asking God before proceeding.

Do not worship in open view of others with the intention of being noticed by men. Do it for the glory of our Father.

Where my heart is, so will my treasure be.

The Lamp of the Body

"The lamp of the body is the eye. If therefore your eye is good, your whole body will be full of light. But if your eye is bad, your whole body will be full of darkness. If therefore the light that is in you is darkness, how great is that darkness!" (Matthew 6:19-21)

My eyes are the gateway to my soul. What I look at affects what I show to those around me.

If I concentrate on looking at darkness (sin), then I will be filled with darkness. Satan's attacks on me are continual and relentless. The content I consume and the people I listen to will fill my soul with either good or evil. If a person or a form of entertainment promotes that sin is acceptable—or even worth celebrating—then it is numbing me to the surrounding darkness. Satan's goal will have been achieved in me, and I will spread that to my family, friends, and loved ones.

On the other hand, if I look *intently* at the good things of God, then I will fill myself with light and shine it on others.

Earnestly pray for the wisdom and discernment to separate the truth from the lies that bombard us each day. One of Satan's tricks is to disguise himself as an angel of light, to spread false teachings in an attempt to turn us from the *truth* that comes from Yahweh and Yeshua.

If I study the Word of God, pray for wisdom and discernment, and welcome the Holy Spirit's work in me, then I will *overcome* these lies. My strength is in the Father, the Son, and the Holy Spirit. I cannot do this alone; I *must* accept their help.

The light that fills us will radiate out and touch others. Our kindness, patience, forgiveness, and love are all attributes of our Father in Heaven that can be shown through us.

You Cannot Serve God and Riches

"*No one can serve two masters; for either he will hate the one and love the other, or else he will be loyal to the one and despise the other. You cannot serve God and mammon*" (Matthew 6:24).

Mammon (in Aramaic, *mamona*): material wealth or possessions, especially as having a debasing influence.

This does not mean that I cannot make money or enjoy the life provided by my Father. In this verse, Jesus is speaking about the priorities in my life and the order in which I place them. Does God come first, or does money? I cannot serve both.

If I place Yahweh first, then the Holy Spirit leads me down the correct path. I will give an honest day's work in exchange for an honest day's wage. The wages I earn are from my Father, and how I manage them matters. I have done my fair share of spending frivolously and wasting my earnings in pursuit of material things.

To be honest, I still do this sometimes. Buyer's remorse is a real thing, and it often comes when we realize that we were being selfish, placing our wants before other's needs or vainly searching for satisfaction in material things. However, true and lasting satisfaction can only be found in Yahweh. It is truly awesome to do things for Yahweh, the happiness that arises within you is unmatched.

The money I earn comes from my Father and belongs to Him; therefore, I should use it to further the Kingdom of Heaven and to glorify God *first*. I should tithe, donate to causes that are dear to Yahweh, and volunteer my time for the same causes. This is how I can do my part for Yahweh's Kingdom.

Do Not Worry

"Therefore I say to you, do not worry about your life, what you will eat or what you will drink; nor about your body, what you will put on. Is not life more than clothing? Look at the birds of the air, for they neither sow nor reap nor gather into barns; yet your heavenly Father feeds them. Are you not of more value than they! Which of you by worrying can add one cubit to his stature?

"So why do you worry about clothing? Consider the lilies of the field, how they grow: they neither toil nor spin; and yet I say to you that even Solomon in all his glory was not arrayed like one of these. Now if God so clothes the grass of the field, which today is, and tomorrow is thrown into the oven, will He not much more clothe you, O you of little faith?

"Therefore do not worry, saying, 'What shall we eat?' or 'What shall we drink?' or 'What shall we wear?' For after all these things the Gentiles seek. For your heavenly Father knows that you need all these things. But seek first the kingdom of God and His righteousness, and all these things shall be added to you. Therefore do not worry about tomorrow, for tomorrow will worry about its own things. Sufficient for the day is its own trouble" (Matthew 6:25-34).

Jesus is *not* telling us to sit and wait for Yahweh to drop food and clothing into our laps. He *is* saying that we are to have *faith* that He will provide for our needs. We are to work in such a way that displays God to everyone we meet, including those from whom we accept a wage. In so doing, Yahweh will provide for us. Good, honest work will come our way.

Jesus is teaching us to avoid becoming preoccupied with material things because that will lead us to worship and serve money instead of Yahweh. He is telling us to seek our Father first in all that we do. It *all* matters. Ask Jesus for help and allow Him to take control of your heart and mind so that you can serve Yahweh in a manner that brings glory to Him, not yourself.

When we serve money first, we will go to any length to obtain it. Lying, cheating, and stealing all become acceptable means to the end of serving ourselves. Serving money first causes us to worship the idols of self and material wants. Satan takes control of us, and he continues to tempt us with more opportunities to sin against God.

By *seeking* Yahweh and serving him first, we place other's needs before our own. We find *true* satisfaction in helping others and serving our Father in Heaven. We may not drive a Mercedes, but we can get by with a dependable vehicle that leaves us with enough money left over with which to serve others.

I will pray for wisdom and pause to ask for guidance throughout my day. I will not charge headlong into the day thinking, "I've got this!" I do not!

It is just a little opposite of what the self-help gurus teach. Okay, totally opposite!

But I need to ask myself, "Do I want to listen to the advice of man, who messes everything up and promotes hate and division, or do I want to listen to my Father in Heaven and His Son, my Savior, who teach love?"

It is a choice of life or death.

Do Not Judge

"Judge not, that you be not judged. For with what judgement you judge, you will be judged; and with the measure you use, it will be measured back to you. And why do you look at the speck in your brother's eye, but do not consider the plank in your own eye? Or how can you say to your brother, 'Let me remove the speck from your eye'; and look, a plank is in your own eye? Hypocrite! First remove the plank from your eye, and then you will see clearly to remove the speck from your brother's eye.

"Do not give what is holy to the dogs; nor cast your pearls before swine, lest they trample them under their feet, and then turn and tear you in pieces" (Matthew 7:1-6).

I am a sinner. I am broken. Without Jesus, I am lost. Through the work of Jesus and my belief in it, I am saved by the grace of Yahweh.

I keep repeating this statement because I must place it at the forefront of my mind. Humility comes when I realize the *truth* of this statement. My salvation does not come from what *I* did for myself; it comes from what *Jesus* did for me and the *grace* extended to me by Yahweh.

Through prayer and diligent study of the Word, the Holy Spirit reveals my sins to me. I am (eventually) grateful for this because it allows me to repent and ask for forgiveness. In this way, I can be a humble and effective disciple and an aid to those who are hurting.

I cannot fulfill the Great Commission (Matthew 28:19-20) unless I first look honestly at my own sins. Then, from a position of humility, I can help others find Jesus through their struggles or questions.

When I see someone who is down and out, in pain, or openly sinning, do I look at them from a position of superiority or from a position of empathy? These are questions that we should be asking ourselves and allowing the Holy Spirit to guide us in.

Jesus teaches that humility is of great importance in all that we do for the Kingdom of Yahweh. I cannot point out the sins of others without first pointing out my own. Nor can I judge others without Yahweh judging me in the same manner. Do I really wish to face judgment in the same way that I have judged others? Of course not! If I judge from a position of superiority, then Yahweh, who *is* pure, will judge me from a *truly* superior position. Not my idea of a fun time.

According to gotquestions.org, "A faithful servant of God will see himself as accurately as he sees others. He will recognize his own sinfulness and need for God's mercy—a need he shares with his brothers and sisters in Christ. He will have no reason to consider himself better than others but will follow Paul's teaching to the Philippians: 'Do nothing out of selfish ambition or vain conceit. Rather, in humility value others above yourselves' (Philippians 2:3)" ("What does it mean to judge not lest you be judged?").

In ancient Israel, dogs and swine were considered unclean, and Jesus compared them to those who refuse to hear the Gospel. Do not give your pearls of wisdom to swine. We are to speak the truth of the Gospel to everyone, but if they refuse to hear it or become angered over it, then you should move on and pray for them. Maybe try again later. Our commission is to spread the Gospel—not force people to believe it. There are many people who thirst for the Word of God, and *we need to find them*.

Proverbs 26:11: "As a dog returns to his own vomit, so a fool repeats his folly." (Do not call anyone a fool. Just saying.)

2 Peter 2:22: "Of [false teachers] the proverbs are true: 'A dog returns to its vomit,' and 'A sow that is washed returns to her wallowing in the mud.'"

We will be given the ability to discern to some measure (1 Corinthians 2:15 -16).

I will share the good news of the Gospel with all, both by my actions and by my words.

Keep Asking, Seeking, Knocking

"Ask, and it will be given to you; seek, and you will find; knock and it will be opened to you. For everyone who asks receives, and he who seeks finds, and to him who knocks it will be opened. Or what man is there among you who, if his son asks for bread, will give him a stone? Or if he asks for a fish, will give him a serpent? If you then, being evil, know how to give good gifts to your children, how much more will your Father who is in heaven give good things to those who ask Him! Therefore, whatever you want men to do to you, do also to them, for this is the Law and the prophets" (Matthew 7:7-12).

Ask. Prayer is how we talk to God. It is how we communicate our desires and our needs. But Yahweh is omniscient (having infinite awareness, understanding, and insight). He knows what we want before we ask. So why ask, right? We ask because doing so puts us in personal communication with our Father in Heaven. By reading the Word and communicating with Yahweh, we learn about ourselves and grow in our knowledge and understanding of His character. As we grow, we will feel bad about asking for a fancier car.

Jesus is not saying that I will get everything I ask for when my prayers are motivated by greed, anger, arrogance, or selfish desires. Those prayers will not be answered.

I should pray for others, for a heart for God, for wisdom, and for understanding of Scripture. These will be given.

Seek. "But seek first the kingdom of God and His righteousness, and all these things shall be added to you" (Matthew 6:33).

Seek *His* plan, *His* wisdom, *His* strength. Seek God Himself!

Yahweh's plan for me will be revealed as I pray and study Scripture. His wisdom and His strength will be given to me so that I may carry out His plan, not mine.

Knock. If I want something, and it happens to be behind a door, I should knock (and keep knocking) in humility. This is an action that I take to learn God's way.

I should study Scripture and absorb Jesus' words, actions, and motivations. Jesus never took a step that did not prioritize my salvation. He put Himself aside for you and for me, for our salvation.

According to gotquestions.org, "Ask, seek, knock. Notice the three different senses being considered here. Asking is verbal; Christians are to use their mouths to petition God for their needs and desires. And believers are to seek with their minds—this is more than asking; it is a setting of priorities and a focusing of the heart. To knock involves physical movement, one in which the Christian takes action. Although asking and seeking are of great importance, they would be incomplete without knocking. The apostle John said Christians ought not to love in word alone but with actions also (1 John 3:18). In the same way, it is good to pray and seek God, but if one does not also act in ways that are pleasing to God, all is for naught. It is no accident that Jesus said believers should love God with all their heart, soul, strength, and mind (Luke 10:27)" (What did Jesus mean when He told us to ask, seek, and knock?").

God delights in prayers of faith, and He promises to give us what we need.

We should pray with faith that He will give us what we need, and we should desire to follow our Father in Heaven.

Matthew 7:12 is the Golden Rule. Jesus enriches this simple phrase by making it a positive command. In doing so, He emphasizes that it summarizes all of the ethical principles set forth in the Law and the Prophets.

It is easy for us to say that we love others, but do we show that love in our actions? Yahweh shows us that He loves all of His creation.

The Sermon on the Mount (Warnings)

The Narrow Way

"Enter by the narrow gate; for wide is the gate and broad is the way that leads to destruction, and there are many who go in by it. Because narrow is the gate and difficult is the way which leads to life, and there are few who find it" (Matthew 7:13-14).

Nobody ever said that following this command would be easy. It's simple but not easy.

It's simple because all I need to do is *believe* in Jesus and what He accomplished for me.

It's not easy because I will be hated. Who wants to be hated? Those around me will scoff, speak of me with derision, and persecute me. I am not alone. They hated Jesus first, so who am I to complain if they hate me too? Paul said it best: "For to me, to live is Christ, and to die is gain" (Philippians 1:21).

Satan will tempt me every day with visuals that want to pull my attention away from Jesus. In our world of 24/7 news media and television, it has become even easier for Satan to offer temptation. A huge amount of disinformation bombards us daily, attempting to confuse us and turn our focus toward the secular worldview instead of the Biblical worldview. It is trying to turn us from Yeshua and Yahweh's truth. John 14:6 says, ***"I am the way, the truth, and the life. No one comes to the Father except through me."***

There is only *one* way to the Father and to Heaven. That way is through faith in Jesus Christ and belief that He came to be sacrificed for my sins, that His blood washes me clean and makes me acceptable to Yahweh.

The alternative is to choose the broad, easy path that is more accepted by man. It is the path of *my* good works, self-righteousness, and belief that there are many ways to Heaven. This is the path to Hell.

My focus should always be on what is accepted by Yahweh and what is taught by Jesus, not man. Yahweh gave Jesus the authority to judge mankind (John 5:22-23).

Jesus is unique in that He is both God and man. Who knows us better than He who walked among us? He knows us better than we know ourselves.

By reading and studying Scripture, who I am is revealed to me. It is both uncomfortable and truly wonderful. It is uncomfortable because my sins are revealed. It is truly wonderful because Jesus offers me salvation. One by one, my sins are revealed and are dealt with forever. Never do I have to receive the punishment that I *so* deserve.

However, I am human. I need Jesus every day. Satan's efforts to tempt me will intensify. I need the Holy Spirit and the teaching of the Word inside of me. I will stumble and fall. I will be picked back up so that I can continue forward. I think that "wash, rinse, repeat" might be appropriate here.

There is no shortcut or easy way to the Kingdom of Yahweh—***"difficult is the way."*** In a world full of so-called "easy" solutions, we can lose our way to our Father. Our walk with Jesus will not be welcomed or supported by most. That is why the road to destruction is broad, and most will go that way.

Revelation describes the Book of Life: "And I saw the dead, small and great, standing before God, and books were opened. And another book was opened, which is the Book of Life. And the dead were judged according to their works, by the things which were written in the books" (Revelation 20:12).

Notice that the verse says "books" (plural, many) and "Book of Life" (singular). If you are following the crowd, it is a clue that you are heading down the broad path to destruction.

Do not *live* for *man*; instead, *spend your life* for Jesus and for the Kingdom of Yahweh.

I have heard of people's lives being described as *"lived to the fullest."* It means that they climbed mountains, traveled the world, or ate in the best restaurants. They experienced adventure and excitement while never having any cares. *Live* spelled backward is *evil*. *Lived* spelled backward is *devil*. Living for self instead of selflessness. Just food for thought.

There are no accidents when it comes to how we spend our lives. It is intentional, whether for good or evil, it's our choice.

The Merriam-Webster definition of *narrow-minded* is "not willing to accept opinions, beliefs, behaviors, etc. that are unusual or different from one's own: not open-minded."

Christians are often called "narrow-minded" in a derogatory way. Well, that is painful. It's expected, but it still hurts. We must lead the conversation with love. Yahweh gives us free will. How we spend eternity is *our choice*. I hope to bring as many people as possible to the Kingdom of Yahweh, but I cannot, and will not, force them. Yahweh doesn't, so how can I? I do this out of my love for Yahweh and Jesus. It is what They want, and I spend my life for Them. If I were to follow my self-interests, then I would remain quiet and keep it to myself. I am a trout fisherman. I enjoy the quiet, far-off places. The less crowded someplace is, the more I enjoy it. Yet, the Kingdom of Yahweh is so much better than anything that is of this world. The glimpses that I have received by the good things that have been gifted me, show me that this promise is true.

Actual narrow-mindedness comes from those who are opposed to God. By *not* changing ourselves to fit in with the culture, we get canceled. When someone denies God to me and shouts hateful things at me, I am to smile and move on. I say prayers for them out of love, not malice.

Satan and the world *hate*. They hate the "narrow way" because it leads to Yeshua and Yahweh and away from Satan.

I will paraphrase Paul: continually train your mind and your heart for Jesus. Read and study the Bible. Become intimately acquainted with Jesus, and through Him, truly come to know and understand Yahweh. Then, go tell others the good news.

According to many scholars, YHWH (we write it *Yahweh*) may mean "He brings into existence whatever exists." If you sound out "YHWH," it sounds to me like a breath. My very breath is both because of and for Yahweh.

The Bible has been proven true, both scientifically and spiritually. Many atheists have tried to prove it wrong but then *became* Christians (e.g., Lee Strobel and J. Warner Wallace). The prophecies in the Bible have come true.

I have read the final chapter. He wins.

I will focus on the *narrow way*—to know Yeshua and to know Yahweh.

You Will Know Them by Their Fruits

"Beware of false prophets, who come to you in sheep's clothing, but inwardly they are ravenous wolves. You will know them by their fruits. Do men gather grapes from thornbushes or figs from thistles? Even so, every good tree bears good fruit, but a bad tree bears bad

fruit. A good tree cannot bear bad fruit, nor can a bad tree bear good fruit. Every tree that does not bear good fruit is cut down and thrown into the fire. Therefore by their fruits you will know them" (Matthew 7:15-20).

Religious *and* political leaders who do not follow the Bible lead their followers down the broad path to destruction.

Jim Jones and David Koresh are just two of the many who have claimed to be prophets and led their followers to destruction. They claimed that they knew of a different path that led to Heaven. They were wrong. There is only one way, and it is narrow and difficult. Churches that advocate for alternative lifestyles and preach that they are acceptable end up leading their parishioners astray. They teach a secular worldview instead of a biblical worldview. Teaching or supporting anything that is not biblical goes against Jesus and Yahweh.

"They are clouds without water, carried about by the winds", Jude 12-13 NKJV, and "These are grumblers, complainers, walking according to their own lusts; and they mouth great swelling words, flattering people to gain advantage." Jude 16 NKJV.

Political leaders who promise a different path, celebrate evil, and do not support the biblical worldview bring about strife, hatred, persecution of Christians, and high costs of living that create more poor citizens and bring arguments over money and morals into our homes. The nations are weakened as they turn away from Yahweh. He turns them over to their perversions, (Romans 1:24-25). He lifts his hand from them. It has happened many times throughout the centuries.

Before the 1960s, the USA was *the* world superpower. With the arrival of the sexual revolution and abortion, we have been on a steady decline ever since.

In our fight for independence, a bunch of God-fearing, Bible-toting farmers kicked what was then the world's superpower out of *our God's* country. A country that was formed on biblical standards. A country that loved and worshiped the one true God and could not be defeated. We have historically been who other countries turned to for help. That is a truth that cannot be denied. Now, we are the laughingstock of the world. That is another truth that cannot be denied.

Just as ancient Israel declined, so are we declining. When Israel turned away from God, other countries attacked and won.

We are not special! We were not chosen and formed by Yahweh as Israel was. We were not powerful; our God was powerful for us. We have turned away from Him and from our support of Israel, ("I will bless those who bless you, and I will curse him who curses you; and in you all the families of the earth shall be blessed." Genesis 12:3), yet we still expect special treatment because we have nice things that rust and decay!

Good fruit comes from a close, personal relationship with our Father and with His Son. A biblical teacher or a politician who has this relationship will display good fruit such as making disciples (Matthew 28:19), humbly doing good (Jeremiah 29:7), and lovingly leading the lost to Jesus (Romans 12:4-8).

Many people will rise to prominence within a church or government who profess faith in Jesus as their Savior, but their lives outside of public scrutiny will proclaim the truth. Greed, lies, and pride will ultimately define them. We are not to judge them, but we are also not to follow them.

I will stand firm in the Word of God and put my faith in Jesus Christ, my Lord and Savior.

I Never Knew You

"Not everyone who says to me 'Lord, Lord,' shall enter the kingdom of heaven, but he who does the will of My Father in heaven. Many will say to Me in that day, 'Lord, Lord, have we not prophesied in Your name, cast out demons in Your name, and done many wonders in Your name?' And then I will declare to them, 'I never knew you; depart from Me, you who practice lawlessness!" (Matthew 7:21-23)

For many, this is the most *chilling* verse in the Bible.

I do not want to imagine Jesus, my Lord, my Savior, my King, turning away from me because I put my faith in myself and in the world instead of in Him. If this is the case, what I have to look forward to is an eternity spent burning alone, in complete darkness, with *all* my memories, and in pain.

This is *not* a pleasant thought. It keeps me up at night.

My faith, salvation, and hope for life are in Jesus Christ who died on the cross for my sins. I cannot be good enough to go to Heaven without faith in Jesus.

My evil thoughts, anger, pride, doubt, and the multitude of things that I do wrong every day cannot be overcome by good works. I can only be presented to Yahweh and cleansed by my faith in Jesus Christ.

Doing good works without faith in Jesus is self-worship. It is believing that I am in control and can get to Heaven on my own. *Actual* good works come from the realization of what Jesus accomplished for me on the cross. I want to do good for others and for Yahweh, not for me.

"Then they said to Him, 'What shall we do, that we may work the works of God?" Jesus answered and said to them, *'This is the work of God, that you believe in Him who He sent'"* (John 6:28-29).

Yahweh's will for us is to believe in Yeshua, His Son, and our Savior. To believe in the salvation rendered to us by Jesus and the grace of forgiveness given by Yahweh.

All sin is lawlessness, or rebellion against the Law of God. Being human and weak, I will sin. I need Jesus Christ in order to be saved.

Build on the Rock

'Therefore whoever hears these sayings of Mine, and does them, I will liken him to a wise man who built his house on the rock: and the rain descended, the floods came, and the winds blew and beat on that house; and it did not fall, for it was founded on the rock.

But everyone who hears these sayings of Mine, and does not do them, will be like a foolish man who built his house on the sand: and the rain descended, the floods came, and the winds blew and beat on that house; and it fell. And great was its fall.'

"And so it was, when Jesus had ended these sayings, that the people were astonished at His teaching, for He taught them as one with authority, and not as the scribes" (Matthew 7:24-29).

In life, stuff happens. Sometimes it's bad stuff, like arguments with loved ones, sickness, death, divorce, or the constant barrage of temptation to sin. These are the rains, floods, and winds of life.

Suffering is universal. Jesus suffered. He set the example for all of us to follow. Through our pain, our Father is still at the center of the universe. The one true God of love who we can trust regardless of how things appear.

By establishing the foundation of my life on the rock of my Lord and Savior Jesus Christ, I will be able to weather the storms of this world. I will be beaten and tossed about, but I will not perish, for my faith is in Jesus.

I will not be protected from trials; I will be taken by the hand and walked through them as I worship Yahweh and learn to trust Him.

There are the daily trials, and there are many more to come. Anything that is taught by the world but goes against the teachings of the Word of God presents a trial that we as Christians must stand through with the strength that we receive from our Father, His Son, and the Holy Spirit.

Satan will attack us continually, and from time to time, we will stumble. We cannot stumble on purpose. We cannot intentionally sin because of our trust in salvation. Sinning with intent is equivalent to calling Jesus a liar. If a bad thought creeps in or a cross word slips out, then realize it, admit it, and ask for forgiveness. It will be given.

Planning to sin today and ask for forgiveness tomorrow does not work. That is making Jesus small and putting ourselves first. And we are not guaranteed tomorrow.

"Do not boast about tomorrow, for you do not know what a day may bring" (Proverbs 27:1, NIV).

Our lives are in Jesus Christ. Each day should be approached as if it is our last.

Jesus Christ introduced us to the God that is written about in the Old Testament. The God that loves His creation so deeply that He continually sent prophets to guide and to call His people back to Him. His love is extended to all His creation by allowing us free will. Yahweh allows us to choose our eternal destiny but with ample warning and descriptions of an eternity spent without Him. No matter how much pain our choices cause Him, they are still ours to make. He has never lied to us, nor has He gone back on His promises. He cannot allow sin in His presence. Yahweh loves us so much that He sent Jesus to be our perfect sacrifice so that if we believe in the Son, we are saved and are gifted righteousness, to spend eternity in the presence of our Father and our Lord and Savior. Then we spend our life for the Kingdom of Yahweh.

"Beloved, let us love one another, for love is of God; and everyone who loves is born of God and knows God. He who does not love does not know God, for God is love. In this the love of God was manifested toward us, that God has sent His only begotten Son into the world, that we might live through Him. In this is love, not that we loved God, but that He loved us and sent His Son to be the propitiation (atonement) for our sins. Beloved, if God so loved us, we also ought to love one another." 1 John 4:7-11 NKJV.

Before Jesus, approaching Yahweh was unheard of. The Jewish Religion taught that He was unapproachable. "The worship instructions in Leviticus were like a manual on handling radioactive material", (The Jesus I Never Knew, Philip Yancey). On the cross, as recorded in Mark, as Jesus breathed His last, "The curtain of the temple was torn in two from top to bottom." This huge curtain separated and blocked off The Most Holy Place where the presence of Yahweh dwelled. No longer was access to Yahweh limited. It was available to everyone who believes in Jesus Christ.

The Apostle Paul called Jesus, "the image of the invisible God." (Colossians 1:15 NIV) Jesus Christ is Yahweh's exact replica. "For God was pleased to have all His fullness dwell in Him" (Colossians 1:19-20 NIV).

"Jesus presents a God with skin on whom we can take or leave, love or ignore. In this visible, scaled-down model we can discern God's features more clearly." And, Jesus is, "brilliant, untamed, tender, creative, slippery, irreducible, paradoxically humble. Jesus stands up to scrutiny. He is who I want my God to be." (The Jesus I Never Knew, Philip Yancey).

The good things that we do in this world are gifts given to us so that we can see and feel a minute portion of the Kingdom of Yahweh.

The guilt, shame, and fear that we feel when committing a sin, or supporting sin, is a minute glimpse of an eternity spent away from our Father.

My Testimony

Jesus truly does pursue us.

I did not grow up in a Christian environment. I knew that God existed, but I did not know Him, nor had I ever heard of Jesus. I grew up on a hardscrabble Kansas farm in the 1960s and 70s. We had no running water or A/C, and we heated our home with wood. We grew rocks and kids, and there were a bunch of both. It was not the best environment to learn about God. I learned about hard work, but little else. But God said, **"I will put My law in their minds and write it on their hearts"** (Jeremiah 31:33).

I knew the difference between right and wrong. My parents and grandparents saw to that. I treated everybody the same. I did not intentionally hurt anybody. I should have been safe, right? I thought so. I believed in God. I didn't know His name, but I believed in Him. I did all these good things. People told me that I was humble and nice. I felt secure and proud that I was going to Heaven, even though my only exposure to the idea of Heaven came during Vacation Bible School where I drew pictures of it. I did not understand Heaven, but I was reassured that all would be revealed to me upon my arrival. I had yet to hear of Jesus. Wow!

I drank and partied prodigiously (for my friends who I hope will read this, that means *a lot*...had to get out the dictionary for that one). I chased girls, experimented with drugs, and broke many laws—both man's and God's. I did all of this while still feeling secure in my eternal destiny. Yes, I knew about eternity. I don't know how or when, but I remember knowing that it was the truth when I heard it. And then I met a girl.

She was a wonderful girl. She had witnessed her mom's murder and was in great pain. I don't believe that I was any help to her. She went to church, and she told me about God. I would wait for her to get out of church and then we would go out. I didn't think I needed to go to church because that was where people who didn't believe in God went. Again, wow!

I slowly started changing the trajectory of my life. I still wasn't searching for God, but I was changing. I joined the Navy to get some semblance of order in my head and so I could provide for that girl who had become my fiancé. She was killed in a car accident while I was away at training. That was when I first found out that she was also pregnant.

The downward spiral was real. On the outside, I was fine. I finished at the top of my class. I was selected for honor duty. I had all the stuff that man looks for. Inside, I was devastated and angry. I sought solace in bars, fights, and women, all of which went against God's desires. I brought hurt and pain to those around me and didn't care. I was led by my selfish desires. I didn't voice it, but I was so deeply angry with Him. Because I did not voice or deal with my thoughts and feelings, I was blind to the damage that it was causing. I had shoved it deep so that *I* could function. I missed her and did not understand why a loving God would take her and my unborn baby from me. I was angry with God. I still believed in Him, but I still did not know Jesus.

Then I got the chance to join a Naval Special Warfare Unit, SBU-22. Awesome! I thought it would be a place to get out my anger and hurt. *Nope.*

God, in His infinite wisdom and love, kept me from being deployed to someplace where there was a chance that I might do something that would prevent me from returning to Him. I know that now.

Through the years, I have intentionally sinned—not out of disbelief, but out of anger and defiance. *I* would dictate the path of my life. Once again, *nope*.

God's infinite grace, mercy, and love kept chasing me. Then Jesus introduced Himself to me. I had a stroke.

Within thirty minutes of having a full-blown stroke (doctor's words), I was fully recovered. *I* took the credit for that because I had no plaque in my arteries, good cholesterol, and good blood pressure. I was in shape, didn't smoke, and had stopped drinking. I bragged that my constitution was like a mule's and that I was invincible. Then I had another stroke. He got my attention.

In the three years between the strokes, I met a woman (who is now my awesome wife). She talked to me seriously about God and about Jesus. I started attending church with her on a regular basis. The pastors were awesome. I believed some, I studied some, and I prayed some, but my pride and sin were still there.

When the second stroke happened, I had double vision and went deaf. I cried, **"FATHER PLEASE!"** That was the last right thing I did. About three hours later, (this delay was my fault), I was finally in the hospital when they discovered the clot that was in my brain stem. They notified my family. That's never good.

Four days later, I *walked* away from the hospital because of **Yahweh**, not because of me. In the doctor's words again, "the worst type of stroke known" had happened to me. The doctor told me that I should have been dead or in a wheelchair. I went back to my work doing HVAC (repairing heating and air conditioning) within sixty days. I have a ringing in one ear and a heaviness in the corner of one eye, but most importantly, *I have Jesus*.

I would *so* happily do it again! I saw the light—not the tunnel, but the pure, white light. I cannot come up with any description of the light other than pure. It permeated everything. I felt the serenity, peace, and love that we all search for. I have found in my studies that I am not alone in seeing or feeling this. I have also discovered that I am not special. He speaks to and reveals himself to all. We only need to listen and quiet ourselves to be able to see Him in His creation. Our Creator and our Savior do not hide from us. We have only to look and to listen.

It took me a while to search for understanding about what happened to me. I dove into His Word. My sins have been revealed to me, and I have been forgiven. I am no longer angry; I only want others to see and feel what I saw and felt. I now know that my wonderful former fiancé and our baby are in the arms of Jesus. They are safe and content, no longer sad or in pain. I also believe it was His plan to comfort her and to save me.

Jesus brought me back to my Father!

I have been forgiven of much! The only reason that I can find for this is that He loves me. If I can be loved and forgiven by Yahweh after what I have done to Him, *anybody* can be forgiven.

I am not perfect. My sin is still within me, but now I can see it clearly. The violence that I am capable of comes from my carnal self. My pride, arrogance, and selfishness are all there, but now they are so much easier to avoid. They are no longer my first choices for a response, and I can ask for forgiveness immediately with assurance that it is given. Happiness and love have taken the place of the anger that dwelt within me for so long.

Any *good* that I have done or will do has always been the result of *Jesus* working overtime to save me, to bring me before our Father, cleansed of my sin, and perfected by my Lord and Savior. He has never given up on me. Jesus never gives up on anyone. Jesus is continually knocking on the door. Good is, (as said earlier), a gift from Yahweh so that we can experience a glimpse of what eternity holds in store for us.

I am *not* good. My God is good.

My prayers now, for my growth in the Way is to arrive in Heaven, out of breath, bruised, and wearied from doing my job. Spreading the good news of Jesus.

Apologetics

I have studied many sources and would like to share a little of what I have learned from them.

The theory of evolution (yes, it is just a theory) states that one animal *kind* can evolve into a different *kind.* The kinds are not species. Species are different humans, animals, and plants within a family or kind. This theory is based on animals (like birds) that change through natural selection; they do not *evolve into different kinds.*

A bird kind, a dog kind, or any other kind can adapt to the specific geographical location in which they live so they can thrive in that environment. They adapt. They do not change kinds (e.g., lizard to bird or pond scum to man). The genetic (digital) code, or DNA, that is available to the kind of animal is not added to; it is subtracted from.

For example, animals that are best suited to cold climates, such as those with long fur, pass on their DNA for long fur to subsequent generations while the DNA that is not suited for that climate (i.e., short fur) is lost. It's a process of subtraction, not addition. If they cannot adapt, they either move or perish. Nothing is added to them. No matter how much they change, they only have the DNA of their *kind* to work with.

You cannot breed a horse and a cow. Nothing will happen because they are different kinds. It has been attempted. You can breed a horse and a donkey because they are of the same kind. The result is a mule, which is a kind of horse—not a *different* kind.

Natural selection is observable and provable. Evolution is a theory because it cannot be observed or proven. If evolution were a fact, it would be happening right before our eyes. Every animal *kind* would be evolving into a human *kind*. The 1ˢᵗ Law of Thermodynamics states that nothing new can be created. We have everything that will ever be available right in front of us.

In Genesis, two of every *kind* were brought onto the Ark, *not* two of every species of animal. Through natural selection, the differences in kinds came about.

I can move to a completely different climate and adapt to it. I will pass on my DNA traits that thrive in that climate. This is a matter of natural selection, not evolution into different kinds.

The many differences between human and animal kinds can be traced to environmental needs. Although humans are all different, we are of the same kind, the human *kind*. The theory of evolution teaches that we are different kinds because we look different. Therefore, we *evolved* differently. This leads to division.

The theory of evolution cannot account for human morality, nor can it account for the obvious design characteristics of DNA, a digital code. When our bodies become ill, our DNA mutates to fight the illness, after we heal, it mutates back to the original form. I did not get that ability from pond scum. My God designed it in me.

DNA studies have proved that mankind descended from two people several thousand years ago. These studies can be found on many secular websites; however, they say 100 to 200 thousand years ago. What they do not say is that the research says, 'just a few thousand years. Taking the measurements of mutations in our DNA and going backwards with the math reveals the short time that mankind has been around. It also shows the dispersal of mankind originated somewhere between North Africa and the Middle East. Just as the Bible says. (Robert Carter, PhD – Marine Biologist, *Is Genesis History?*) Another thing that Mr. Carter points out is truly amazing. The mutations of our DNA are counted as loss of DNA. The lighter skin, hair, and eyes are DNA *loss*, not *gain*. It came about from environmental needs.

This is science.

Creation is another bit of science.

The majority of scientists have finally arrived at the conclusion that the universe started all at once. They call it the Big Bang Theory. They cannot prove how it happened; they just know that it did. The credit has yet to be given to Yahweh (hence, the label of "theory"). There is no evidence to further the idea that the universe gradually came into being over millennia. It happened all at once.

Only a force that exists outside of space, time, and matter could be an *uncaused first cause*. The vast amount of power that could bring our universe into existence can only come from our God, Yahweh.

Nothing that exists could have caused itself to exist.

Something cannot come from *nothing*—*unless* it has a push like what is described in Genesis.

Let's say you set up a row of dominoes. If left alone, their state will not change. They will just sit there inanimately. If you push the first one, they will all move. Imagine that. It takes action from an outside force to get them to do something.

The universe also appears as being *fine-tuned* to support life. According to Steven Hawking, (Black Holes and Baby Universes and Other Essays. New York: Bantam, 1993, Google eBook, chapter 7), "If the proton-neutron mass difference were not about twice the mass of the electron, one would not obtain the couple of hundred or so stable nuclides that make up the elements and are the basis of chemistry and biology."

Atoms appear to be fine-tuned and calibrated just right so that life can exist.

If the earth were slightly different in size, at a different distance from the sun, in a different orbit, or experienced any multitude of slight differences, life would not be possible.

Life is designed, and it requires an incredibly intelligent and powerful designer.

If we look at the order of creation, we can see the obvious signs of design that would not have been obvious to ancient people. Light first, then dry land and sea, then plants, then animals, and last He created man to have dominion over it all. Light for energy, land for fertile soil, plants for photosynthesis, (without which nothing could survive), and lastly animals and man which rely on all that came before. When Genesis was recorded, no science existed to explain these facts. Moses relied on Yahwehs expert, firsthand account of creation.

Once again, He designed it, and He defines it.

Scholars date the book of Job to before 2100 BC, (the oldest book in the Bible), just before the time of the patriarchs (Abraham, born around 2166 BC), Isaac, and Jacob. Also, within the pages are clues to the timeframe. Job's age of 200 years, the Chaldeans who raided him had not formed Babylon yet, Job's wealth was in livestock instead of gold, Adam and the Noahic flood are mentioned but not Abraham, Israel, the Exodus, and the law of Moses). Job and his friends were more followers of the one true God before Israel was formed. Job lost all his wealth and family. He accused God of being unjust and unkind. Yahweh challenged Job's authority and power with His own.

"Canst thou bind the sweet influences of Pleiades, or loose the bands of Orion? Canst thou bring forth Mazzaroth in his season? or canst thou guide Arcturus with his sons?" (Job 38:31-32, KJV)

This verse mentions four constellations: Pleiades, Orion, and Arcturus are known to us, but Mazzaroth has yet to be discovered. Maybe a comet that appears only occasionally?

Pleiades ("bind the sweet influences of Pleiades") is an open star cluster consisting of 250 individual stars that are approximately the same age and have roughly the same chemical composition. They are bound together by mutual gravitational attraction. All 250 stars move together as one, drifting through space in unison. They appear the same today as they did in 2100 BC, just as Yahweh described.

Orion ("loose the bands of Orion") refers to the three stars that make up the belt of the Orion constellation: Alnilam, Mintaka, and the cluster Alnitak. Two remain in place, while the third is moving away—loosening the belt, just as Yahweh described. There is no way that Job knew this truth without being told by Yahweh. It cannot be seen with the naked eye.

Arcturus ("guide Arcturus with his sons") is one of the brightest stars in the night sky. It is also a runaway star that is thousands of times larger than our sun. Fifty-two additional stars (his sons) are connected directionally with Arcturus. Charles Burckhalter of the Chabot Observatory said, "these stars are a law unto themselves. Arcturus is one of the greatest suns in the universe, is a runaway whose speed of flight is 257 miles per second." (Cold Case Christianity and Wonder Worlds). Our sun moves at a rate of 12.5 miles per second. This discovery occurred in 1971 AD, but Job heard it from our God before 2100 BC.

These facts of astronomy were known to the ancient world because they were taught by Yahweh, not because they were discovered by modern science. Modern science was born from Christianity to seek out God's truth. Secular science weakly tries to argue against the sovereignty of Yahweh.

Many more scientific facts are in Job such as, Earth's rotation, (first theorized in 1543 A.D. by man), springs of the sea, (discovered in 1977 A.D.), the way of light, (1886 A.D. electromagnetic radiation).

The author of Job has been suggested to be either Moses or Solomon. Moses is a good choice because his father-in-law was Jethro, who was a priest of Midian, (Midianites were descended from

Abraham and his wife Keturah), and this could have been taught to Moses. (Jethro was also called Reuel which means "friend of God". This probably means that he was a priest of The Most High God, which would account for his support of Moses and his help to Israel). The Midianites were a nomadic people in the Arabian Desert. They were children of Abraham. Jethro was another priest of Yahweh before Israel was formed.

There are two video series called *Is Genesis History?*, and *The Days of Noah*. In them, archeologists and geologists explain how there is evidence of the flood. It is compelling information that can be helpful when *discussing* (not arguing) biblical truth.

They both show the Grand Canyon (and much more, but I will stick to this). The different observable layers are flat and even, like layers of a cake. These layers are found around the world, and at the same elevations. Mainstream science says that these layers were separated by millions of years. One of the problems with this 'theory' is that it does not consider the effects of erosion by rain or wind. Yet, they say that dinosaurs lived then. I guess they did not need to eat or drink. And what about the dinosaurs and trees that have been found within multiple layers (search for images of fossilized trees in multiple layers on the internet)?

Another problem with their theory is The Schnebly Hill formation that is just north of The Grand Canyon. In the Grand Canyon this formation is missing, yet it appears about seventy miles to the north. It is situated between the Coconino Sandstone and the Hermit Formations. In the Grand Canyon, secular science says there are roughly 10 million years between the Coconino and Hermit. So how did the Schnebly Hill formation fit in there, and why is it missing from the Grand Canyon? If a catastrophic flood that covered everything had happened, that would answer the question.

More questions arise from mainstream science than answers. The video series ***Is Genesis History?*** is available on YouTube.

Place some dirt and sand into a jar of water. Stir it all up and let it set for a while before observing how *quickly* the different layers are formed.

Secular scientists use radioactive isotope dating to age the different layers of rocks. With this method, they get ages in the millions of years. Three samples were sent to a major secular lab from the Institute for Creation Research team. These three samples were from the eruption of Mt. St. Helens which happened in 1980. The first came back as 240,000 years old, the second was 250,000 years old, and the third was 3,000,000 years old (ICR.org). Hmmm. Rocks that were tested from volcanic eruptions that the dates of the eruptions were known also returned with millions of years ages. If anything does happen to come back with a young age, it is rejected because it does not fit the narrative of an old Earth. Presupposed belief in the Earth being billions of years old causes anything pointing to Biblical historicity as truth to be cast aside.

The oldest known living tree is a bristlecone pine in eastern California named Methuselah. It has been dated using dendrochronology (counting tree rings). Pines can sometimes skip a year or have multiple rings in one year; however, it is still a reliable and close method for dating pine trees. The tree has been aged at 4,853 years old, give or take some years. The biblical timeline for the flood is 4,359 years ago. If what scientists say about dating pine trees is true, Methuselah dates to the days of the flood. Maybe this is the first tree to sprout after the Flood?

I have a personal thought on the flood. Before the flood, the earth was described like a biosphere. There were no mountains, thunderstorms, earthquakes, or any sickness or death. It was beautiful. The firmament (land) was not separated, (Pangaea). Dr. Kurt Wise, in *Is Genesis History?*, explains a computer model that shows that at the time of the destruction of the world, the continents broke apart and were moving at the pace of a fast walk, about five miles per hour.

During the flood, water came up from within the earth and down from the sky. Massive eruptions from every volcano in the world, (active and inactive number in the thousands), and earthquakes like we have never witnessed were worldwide. The world was destroyed and reshaped into what we see now. This resulted in the formation of our majestic mountain ranges, oceans, and canyons. Still beautiful.

Our Father's righteous anger produces only beauty. His judgment of us will also produce only beauty. Evil will be gone.

What about dinosaurs? Mainstream science claims that dinosaurs and man did not exist at the same time. The Bible mentions animals that do not exist today. Dinosaurs are not specifically mentioned because that is a relatively new term, (Richard Owen 1841). The Hebrew word used is *tanniyn*, which the King James Version translates as "dragon." It seems to describe a giant reptile. Most civilizations have dragon stories, and many have catastrophic flood stories. At the time of translation, man had no other reference for how to translate the word. "Dragons" appear nearly thirty times in the Old Testament (e.g., Psalm 74:13, Isaiah 27:1, and Jeremiah 14:6) and were mentioned as living both on land and in water. Another Hebrew word is *livyathan*, which is transliterated as *leviathan*. It is mentioned six times (e.g., Job 41:1 and Psalm 104:26) and is described as a large, fierce sea creature. A megalodon or whale? But, "on earth there is nothing like him" (Job 41:33). There's also the *behemoth* (Job 40:15), which is described as a huge, plant-eating animal that dwells by the water. Its "bones are like beams of bronze," its "ribs are like bars of iron," and its "tail [is] like a cedar" (Job 40:17-18). *Brachiosaurus,* anyone? Some say this is a hippopotamus. Look at a picture of a hippo. I personally do not see a tail like a cedar tree or bones like bronze beams.

In the 13th century, Marco Polo described huge serpents in China: "At the fore part, near the head, they have two short legs, each with three claws, as well as eyes larger than a loaf and very glaring. The jaws are wide enough to swallow a man, the teeth are large and sharp, and their whole appearance is so formidable, that neither man, nor any kind of animal can approach them without terror" (*The Travels of Marco Polo*, translation by William Marsden: Book 2, Chapter 49). Look up *velociraptor* or *t-rex*. Some refute this as Marco Polo saw a fossil. A fossil with glaring eyes that struck fear into any who saw it? When was the last time a fossil scared you?

Many depictions of dinosaurs are found in cave drawings and the Nazca Lines that attest to the fact that men saw dinosaurs.

St. George was a Roman soldier who killed a 'dragon' in Silene, (modern Libya). They cut it up and it took four carts to haul the body. When offered a reward he declined, asking only that he be allowed to share the gospel. The entire town converted. Rome executed George because he would not recant the Gospel. Nothing was mentioned about him slaying a mythical creature.

So, what happened to them? Climate change? Lack of food sources? *Or maybe Yahweh's ways are above ours.*

The biosphere (the earth before the flood) was gone, and the forest that covered the earth was obliterated, (coal beds. *Is Genesis History?*). The earth was drying out and warming up. The same continues today. (*I'm not saying that we are not causing damage to our environment; we are. But we are accelerating natural occurrences. We are not caring for our home.*) The 2nd Law of Thermodynamics states that 'the state of entropy (lack of order or predictability; gradual decline into disorder) of the entire universe, as an isolated system, will always increase over time.' Just as the Bible states. Also, if you think about it, the dinosaurs would have been a huge supply of meat.

In his book *Jubal Sackett*, novelist Louis L'Amour described the killing of a mastodon. When challenged, he defended his point in the February 1987 edition of *Western Horsemen*: "The best story of the mastodon, though, is in the ethnographic records of the Smithsonian Institute. They tell about the Ponca Indians, who lived in the vicinity of Yankton, S.D., who used to make what they called The Long Hunt.

. .. On one of these trips, perhaps the last one and it couldn't have been earlier than the 1600s and it very likely was in the 1700s this happened, they killed a mastodon near Niobrara, Nebraska.

"They tell about it, and not only that, they knew him well enough to have a name for him – pasnuta, which in Ponca means 'long nose.'

"Not only the mastodon, they killed something else, they only describe, which had to be a giant ground sloth (supposedly extinct at the time)."

Mr. L'Amour was known for his authentic and painstakingly researched stories. If he wrote about a spring, "it is there, and the water is good to drink." (This statement comes from many of Mr. L'Amour's books. He wrote his stories after researching and exploring the country that he wrote about.)

It is a recent discovery, (according to National Center for Science Education, a secular publication. March 25, 2005, edition of Science, Mary Schweitzer), that there is soft tissue and intact blood vessels in dinosaur bones. This speaks of recent death, not millions of years. Yeast has been taken from what was supposedly 40,000,000-year-old amber, and then it was used to make beer. ??? Bacteria and worms from the ocean floor that are found in the Cambrian layer are also found alive today. (Creation.com)

It takes perfect conditions to form fossils. If bones are left exposed for any length of time, scavengers and the elements decay and remove the bones. The same goes for fossilized tracks. Tracks are made in mud and do not remain for long. Ask any hunter who has attempted trailing an animal in the rain. The tracks are not discernable after a short time. Or take a walk on a beach and see how long the tracks last. All fossils are the result of being rapidly covered by sediment, such as you would expect in a catastrophic event such as the Flood in Genesis.

I encourage you to watch the movie on YouTube, *Is Genesis History?*. Listen to the scientists, geologists, archeologists, and biologists that offer accurate evidence and explanations for what we observe every day, and of recent discoveries within the science community.

Yahweh has left evidence for us to see the truth.

Our preconceived notions may cause us to disregard written, verifiable, historic documents that do not agree with the secular worldview. Historians are held in low regard by "scientists," especially when the historian has firsthand accounts that do not agree with the scientist's theories. These accounts spoke of things that have only recently been discovered by science. Yet, the scientists say that historians are wrong. In my opinion, this does not quite add up. Repeatedly, the Bible has been proven to be historically true and valid.

Archaeological finds:

• Dead Sea Scrolls (Qumran, Israel, 1947-56): proved the reliability of the transmission process for Bible texts.

• Taylor Prism (Ninevah, Iraq, 1830): corroborated the campaigns of Sennacherib found in 2 Kings 18:13-19, 2 Chronicles 32:1-12, and Isaiah 36:1-38

• House of David Inscriptions (Tel Dan, Israel, 1993-94): contain the earliest extra-biblical mention of King David, who some secular scholars claim is a fictional character.

• Sargon Inscriptions (Khorsabad, Iraq, 1843): confirmed the existence of Sargon, King of Assyria (Isaiah 20:1) and his conquering of Samaria (2 Kings 17:23-24)

- Epic of Gilgamesh (Nineveh, Iraq, 1853): first extra-biblical find that appears to reference the great flood of Genesis 7-8

- Weld-Blundell Prism (Babylon, Iraq, 1922): contains a list of Sumerian Kings with extraordinary long-life spans.

The long-life spans that are recorded in the Bible and the shortened lifespans now can be accounted for with the 2nd Law of Thermodynamics. Man was created perfect and made to live forever. In the Garden, sin was introduced. The further history has progressed, entropy has become the common rule. Lifespans shortened. There are many, many more finds that prove the Bible's historical accuracy.

Yet, the Bible is still dismissed as myth because it does not agree with the secular worldview. But truth is truth whether it is identified as such or not.

The Bible is the written reality of Yahweh's love for His creation. It is the story of Yeshua, our Savior and our King. It is the history of mankind. It is also the story of Yahweh's pursuit of His creation. His continual asking us to turn back to Him and be saved.

When studied, the Bible obscures the false gods and sends them off to wander the wastelands (Matthew 12:43-45).

Every major civilization to exist has fallen. They worshiped false gods. Their histories should be studied as testaments to what happens to those who worship Yahweh and those who don't. When the sins are complete, destruction comes.

Personally, I find this all to be stimulating and intriguing. But I *love* history. None of this information is a point of contention, either with other Christians or with non-believers. It provides a basis for discussion, for meaningful *talks*. Arguing whether dinosaurs existed alongside man is not going to bring anyone to Jesus. However, it is a possible point to address with non-believers who believe only in scientific evidence. Evidence against the secular worldview has either been removed or shut down. If their view of science can be called into question, maybe they will ask to see our evidence found in the Bible. Anything is possible with the Holy Spirit.

My thought is that belief in the beginning of the Bible leads to belief in the ending of the Bible. Satan attempts to make us not believe in the beginning so that will lead us to not believe in the ending. We will exchange the truth for the lie.

Do not argue these points; instead, present them with love and respect. If you are going to use this information, do more research for yourself. I just touched on them here. There is much more to be learned.

We are to present the Gospel in a loving manner, accompanied by the humility that comes from the realization of our sinful natures and our dependence on the saving grace of Yahweh through the work accomplished for us by Yeshua.

We are saved through belief in Jesus and faith in His works. Jesus came to earth from Heaven, lived a sinless life, was sacrificed for our sins, was raised from the dead, and then (after being seen by many) ascended to Heaven to take His place at the right hand of Yahweh. We are washed clean of our sins through the blood of Jesus Christ and are presented as acceptable to Yahweh.

This is the good news that we are to share unashamedly with the world through our actions and words. *Everybody* has this salvation available to them! This offer of salvation is withheld from no one—***no person, not anybody***! We are all in the same boat. We choose our eternal destinies. Yahweh gives us free will to choose eternal life with Him or eternal suffering without Him. It's our choice.

We are to repent of our sins, ask for forgiveness, be made acceptable to Yahweh by our belief in the life, death, and resurrection of our Lord and Savior Jesus Christ, and then share the Gospel. *Those* are our marching orders.

We cannot force others to believe; that is between them and Yahweh. Our job is to represent.

The Bible is supported by science, archeology, and our consciences. There are many resources available to help us learn how to present these truths in a knowledgeable manner. It is difficult to ask someone to believe if we do not have the facts to back it up.

So, read and understand the Bible and search out the evidence that is all around you. (*Have situational awareness – be aware of God's presence in the wind, flowers, or a smile.*) Invest in quality study materials such as a study Bible in your favorite translation, an atlas of the Bible, a Bible dictionary, and a concordance.

Go into battle equipped to present the truth in a kind, loving, and humble manner.

Love your neighbor in the same way that you wish to be loved.

Give generously of all your resources.

Present your life in such a way that shows you are a follower of Yeshua and that you worship the one true God, Yahweh.

The Kingdom of Yahweh is within me. Yahweh is love, and I am to show His love to others.

Yahweh alone is holy (this is *exclusive* to Him). Yahweh offers forgiveness (this is *inclusive*, available to everybody).

In the eyes of our Lord, we are all the same. There is no caste system or prejudice.

The Apostles came from varying backgrounds. Some, such as Paul, had power and prestige. He was a Pharisee, a Roman citizen, and came from a connected family. Luke was a physician. They all gave up their possessions and social standing for the Gospel because they knew the truth of Jesus firsthand. Paul and many others went to their deaths because they would not deny Jesus. They spent their lives proclaiming the salvation of Jesus as they tried to bring others to Christ. Paul was imprisoned multiple times, stoned and left for dead, shipwrecked, and ultimately beheaded, all while proclaiming the truth of Jesus Christ.

*People **do not** die for lies.*

Becoming a Christian in the early days of the Church did not come with any perks. The early Christians were cut off, excluded from business dealings, and denied by their families. Yet, they followed Jesus anyway—not for worldly reasons, but because He was the truth.

Against all odds, Christianity grew in the face of fierce persecution. Walter Wink said, "Killing Jesus was like trying to destroy a dandelion head by blowing on it." (Walter Wink quotes, quotefancy.com)

Many are preaching about the end times, which is good because those things need to be shared. Things are happening in the world at a much faster pace. 'wars and rumors of wars' (Matthew 24:6-13 NIV). But we also need to teach about the beginning. We need to lay a strong foundation. When we believe in the beginning, the end becomes clear.

Our job as Christians is to make disciples. We all have different strengths when it comes to evangelizing (teaching, writing, speaking, etc.). We cannot all be like Billy Graham or Lee Strobel. Talking to one person is just as important as preaching to thousands. It all matters.

The Christian genealogy of Billy Graham started with a Sunday School teacher by the name of Edward Kimball in 1858 who brought Dwight L. Moody to Christ. From there it progressed to Frederic Meyer, Wilbur Chapman, Billy Sunday, and Mordecai Ham. Ham held a crusade in Charlotte, North Carolina in 1932 where 16-year-old Billy Graham gave his life to Christ. Accept Jesus, find your niche, live according to the Law, and share the Gospel. That Sunday School teacher has been responsible for saving an untold number of souls.

Here's some more apologetics (which is Greek for "defense of").

Jesus' death and resurrection

Many critics of Christianity claim that crucifixions did not happen, or if they did happen, that Jesus survived and left the tomb by Himself. We will use Alexander Metherell, M.D., PH.D. found in Lee Strobels' book, The Case For Christ to refute, (with modern medicine), the critics, beginning on page 193.

Jesus sweated blood the night before His crucifixion. This is a medical condition known as, *hematidrosis.* Under extreme psychological stress, the human body has been known to release chemicals that break down the capillaries in the sweat glands, allowing a small amount of blood to infuse the sweat or tears. It also sets up the skin to be extremely fragile just a few hours before He was severely flogged.

Roman floggings were brutal, sadistic affairs that were unlike any others. The flogging typically consisted of thirty-nine lashes using a whip of braided leather thongs with metal balls and sharp pieces of bone woven into it. The metal balls softened and bruised the skin while the bone cut deep lacerations. The spine and ribs would be exposed and sometimes the internal organs were also laid bare. The whipping was from the shoulders down the back, the buttocks, and the legs. Many died before being crucified because of the severity. Jesus was in *hypovolemic* shock due to the amount of blood loss. It is where the heart is racing, trying to pump blood that is not there, blood pressure drops, kidneys stop working, and the person becomes very thirsty. Jesus was so severely beaten that He could not carry the beam, Simon of Cyrene had to. Later Jesus said, "I thirst."

At Golgotha, Jesus was laid down and stretched out so that spikes, five to seven inches long, could be driven through His wrists, (in the language of the day the wrist was considered part of the hand). The spikes were driven through the median nerve. The pain described by

Metherell was if you took a pair of pliers and squeezed and twisted your funny bone, that would be close to what Jesus experienced on both wrists and His feet. The pain was so intense that no word had existed to describe it, so they came up with a new one. *Excruciating,* it literally means, '*out of the cross*.' His shoulders were stretched so that they were out of joint, which fulfilled Psalm 22, which foretold the crucifixion hundreds of years before it happened, 'My bones are out of joint.' Then he was hung in a vertical position, creating the cross.

Stretched out and hanging vertically, the body is held in the exhale position. To breathe, the individual had to raise themselves up with their nailed feet, causing even more damage to the feet. When total exhaustion had set in, the individual died of asphyxiation.

As the breathing slows, *respiratory acidosis* happens. This is carbon dioxide in the blood that dissolves as carbonic acid, causing the blood to increase in acidity, which leads to irregular heartbeat and cardiac arrest.

So, asphyxiation, heart attack, or massive blood loss, either way, nobody was coming off the cross alive. If anyone *were* to live, it would be weeks, months, or longer before they could function at a lesser degree than before.

Before He died, Jesus had some other things going on inside of His body. The hypovolemic shock would have caused a rapid heart rate, resulting in fluid being gathered around the heart and lungs. This is called pericardial effusion and pleural effusion respectively. John reports in his Gospel, that blood and water came out of the wound caused by the Roman spear being thrust into Jesus to make sure that He was dead. The only way that would have happened was if Jesus was truly dead.

The medical knowledge available at the time would not have known this small, but important fact. Now maybe, just maybe, this was told to us in scripture (the living word of God), so that we who are *so* wise, could see the truth.

The Roman soldiers were under compulsion to make sure the crucified individuals were actually dead, and they were professional soldiers whose job was death. If they allowed anyone to live, *they* would suffer the penalty of death. The legs of the other two criminals were broken so that they would die sooner. This fulfilled another prophecy in Psalm 34:20.

To the critics who say that crucifixion did not happen, archaeology has proven that it happened as it was told. In 1968, a victim of crucifixion was unearthed in Jerusalem with the seven-inch nail still in his feet. Another was found in the UK. It happened as it has been reported. Both in the Bible, and in non-biblical historical writings.

Jesus appeared on Resurrection Sunday, (the third day), fully healed. Before the crucifixion, the Apostles were fearful and in hiding. Peter denied knowing Jesus three times before the rooster crowed. After His resurrection, the Apostles could not be stopped. They boldly and fearlessly proclaimed the good news of Jesus. When told by the Jewish authorities to speak no more of Jesus, Peter said that he could not stop spreading the good news. He did not stop until he was crucified upside down in Rome. All went to their deaths proclaiming Jesus and His resurrection.

When viewed from a medical perspective, Jesus 'suffering the cross' for us, takes on a whole new meaning. A deeper understanding of just what He endured for *us*. He did not *have* to, He chose to go through this humiliation, ridicule, suffering, and excruciating pain, *for us*. His love for us is so great, that He laid down His life, so that we may live.

The Gospels

The four Gospels—Matthew, Mark, Luke, and John—are eyewitness accounts of Jesus' life. Their authorship has been questioned by atheists and secularists. *Of course.*

If you were going to write a false story, hoping that it would be believed, wouldn't you attribute it to someone famous, someone with authority?

The fanciful, apocryphal "gospels" were written much later than the Gospels and were falsely attributed to more well-known, exemplary people such as Peter, Mary, and Philip.

Matthew was a despised tax collector. In Israel, the tax collectors worked for Rome and were paid by what they could extort from their fellow Jews. John Mark, (Mark), was not one of the original twelve apostles, he was a companion of Peter and learned from him. Luke, known as Paul's "beloved physician" was also not one of the original twelve. He wrote the Gospel of Luke and Acts, which he learned about from Paul. The author of the Gospel of John is questioned because of Papias. Papias was an early Christian writer and student of John who referred to John the Apostle and John the Elder, but the context of his writing does not make it clear whether he is referring to one man or two. (Yet John referred to himself as the elder in 2 John:1 and again in 3 John:1) Other than that, it is universally acknowledged that John the Apostle, son of Zebedee, wrote the Gospel of John.

Some may argue that the New Testament was written too many years after the events it describes, so the authors' memories could be clouded. This argument is refuted by the story of Paul. Paul (known as Saul at the time) was on his way to Damascus with orders to arrest Christians when he encountered Jesus, was blinded, and converted to Christianity after Jesus revealed the Truth to him (Acts 9:1-19). The men who were accompanying Paul were under the same orders, yet they did not arrest any Christians (or Paul, for that matter), and they took Paul to the Christians. The crucifixion was in 30 AD. Paul's conversion was in 32 AD. After his conversion, he went into Damascus and met with a Christian named Ananias (who healed his blindness) and some other disciples. There, he heard the original creed of the early Christians. Paul met with the apostles around 35 AD and learned more. Jesus' death and resurrection were taught in the earliest creed of the Christian church (we know this for sure because of Paul), and the creed can be confidently dated within two years of the crucifixion. Paul's epistles (letters) quoted from the Gospels and have been dated between AD 48 and AD 60. Evidence for the authenticity of the Gospels can be found in writings of non-believers from the same time period, such as Josephus, Tacitus, Thallus, Mara Bar-Serapion, and Phlegon.

Many claims have been made that Christianity and its beliefs were copied from pagan religions. The claims of miracles and resurrection to be exact. However, the dates that these pagan miracles and resurrections were written are after the Gospels. Also, we have already discovered how everyone knew who Yahweh was and that He was in fact the One True God and how many before the formation of Israel worshipped Yahweh.

Paganism was born from a deliberate attempt to replace Yahweh so that people could chase their carnal desires without worry. Yet, when faced with the truth, they shrunk from confrontation with Israel unless Israel had turned away from Yahweh. Pagans did not fear Israel, they feared Yahweh. Remember, Israel was outnumbered and outgunned.

The pagan religions were based on teachings by man. They promoted a combination of hate and/or praying to multiple gods or even praying to men used to replace pantheons. They used human, (usually children) sacrifices to appease their gods and promoted sexual promiscuity. Violence was used to force people to worship false gods or even men. The pagan religions varied to some degree, but none were even close to worshiping Yahweh and His teachings of love. Remember, Yahweh did not show how to hate others. Nobody had to accept Him unless they chose to. The nation of Israel did not keep on conquering and building an empire as other nations had, both before and after Israel was formed. Yahweh used them to punish Canaan because their sins were complete. The Canaanites could not have gotten any more evil. They had reduced themselves to sacrificing their children.

Pain and Hell

Some argue that a loving God would not condemn His creation to Hell or allow pain in His created world. From my testimony, you can see how this is personal to me, especially the last portion.

Yahweh created a perfect world with no sickness or pain. He also gave humans free will. In their freedom, Adam and Eve chose to rebel against God. Thus, entered sin, pain, suffering, and death. They chose to put themselves before Yahweh.

We are acting in the same manner today. We choose to place ourselves at the highest level of importance. It is a fact of humanity that we place ourselves and our wants at the center of our universe. Selfishness rules. Pain and suffering are rampant in a world that prioritizes our desires above serving others as He intended. We do this, yet we still expect to not be punished.

If every person in the world only concentrated on their own selfish desires, we would have wars, famine, murder, theft, deceit, sexually transmitted diseases, abortions, unwed mothers, absent fathers, oh, wait a minute . . . that *is* what we have. ***People get hurt!*** We have allowed Hell to be present on earth. **WE** did this! This is **OUR** fault!

Yahweh's view of events is pure. When we sin, we cause Him great pain. In our defiance and selfishness, we demand to be left alone and allowed to cause others pain if it makes us feel better.

What does a pure and holy God do with us then? Reward us for harming others? Hell is not a place for good people who did not believe the right way. **None** of us are good! Hell is the reward for unrepentant sinners who do not accept Jesus Christ as their Lord and Savior.

Pride and selfishness are at the root of the problem. If our desires are not met, we say that God doesn't exist because we didn't get what we wanted. If we do get what we want, who goes without a meal or a warm place to sleep? Yahweh protects the innocent. My inability to get that fancy house, because I got passed over for a promotion, might mean that someone else was able to feed their children. These actions of ours are intentional defiance of the Law of God. Yahweh is pure and just. He cannot allow this. As I said earlier, it's not that He *will* not, it's that He *cannot*.

I picture a selfish person standing before Yahweh with their hands on their hips. In defiance, they demand that they be allowed to continue living as they have been. Yahweh is hurt but grants their demand out of His love for them and sends them to spend eternity in Hell, away from His presence. The choice of how we spend eternity is ours to make. ***We choose!***

Many think that they could have more fun without moral laws and the absence of our God. What they do not factor in is that with the absence of Yahweh, there will be no restraint. Humans would reduce themselves to causing as much pain as they choose. Survival of the fittest would rule. We would be reduced to the likeness of the animal kingdom. Sickness, pain, suffering, hunger, and thirst would be the norm. For eternity. With no relief.

We have had glimpses of this in our recorded history and on the daily news, Hitler, Stalin, the abusiveness of the modern slave trade, China, and North Korea to name just a few.

We can choose to adopt attributes like patience, love, and empathy, but we can only *choose* to act on these good attributes. Yahweh did not just adopt good attributes; He is the *definition* of them.

Jesus chose to come to earth, become a man, and become the sacrifice for our sins. **He took our sins upon Himself!** We must only believe and have faith in Him. We cannot heal ourselves; He heals us. He makes us acceptable before Yahweh.

The Bible teaches that there are different levels of rewards in Heaven and punishments in Hell. Jesus has been given the authority to judge. He will be just in His judgments, and no one will be able to say that it was unfair.

I may end up digging a ditch in Heaven, but it will be a ditch that is dug for my Lord, and I will be ecstatic and singing while I dig.

The Truth

Many believe that parts of the Gospels contradict each other and are therefore suspect. However, if we look at the core of the story, they all agree.

For instance, Jesus was buried in a tomb provided by Joseph of Arimathea. Women discovered that the stone had rolled away, and the tomb was empty, indicating the resurrection of Jesus. These are the core agreements about the death and resurrection of Jesus.

Joseph of Arimathea was a member of the Sanhedrin, who were the very people encouraging the crucifixion of Jesus. Luke explains that Joseph was not present for the vote. After Jesus' death, the Apostles had scattered and were in hiding. The only people available to give Jesus an honorable burial were Joseph and Nicodemus (another member of the Sanhedrin). This was reported in all four Gospel accounts, even though it was something that the early Christians would not have been proud of.

A group of women found and reported the empty tomb whose two-ton stone had been rolled away. They also had visions of angels at the tomb. Again, this was reported in all four Gospels. In ancient Israel, women were of low regard. Common sentiment would say something like, "Let the words of the Law be burned rather than delivered to women." Women were not allowed to testify in a Jewish court of law. Yet, all four Gospels reported the testimony of women regarding the empty tomb.

The Apostles and disciples saw Jesus' visible wounds from His crucifixion. The Jewish leaders and Roman authorities never denied that the tomb was empty; they only tried to cover it up. This fact was reported by non-Christian writers.

Nowhere in the New Testament is there mention of the siege of Jerusalem, a prophecy made by Jesus. The fall of Jerusalem was in AD 70 when the Romans tore down the Temple. 'Then, as some spoke of the temple, how it was adorned with beautiful stones and donations, He said, **"These things which you see—the days will come in which not *one* stone shall be left upon another that shall not be thrown down." Matt 24:2.** If the Gospels were written after AD 70, they would have made mention of this prophecy coming true. None of the Gospels make mention of the deaths of James in AD 62, Paul in AD 64, and Peter in AD 65. However, non-Christian historians tell of all these events.

Jesus taught that all were equal in the eyes of our Father. There are no classes or discrimination, and all are loved equally. The Apostles were committed to the truth, regardless of the discomfort it might cause. They were executed while still proclaiming this same truth.

These authors came from different backgrounds and different levels of education. They were also speaking to different groups of people and explaining things so that culturally, they would be understood.

We will step away from apologetics and speak of something that is being taught today.

Slavery

This is kind of a touchy subject. If we look at it from a historical perspective, it was and is wrong. However, it did not exist in the exact way that it is being taught.

At one point in history, *all* countries had slaves. The word *slave* comes from the word *slav,* which was not used until the 9^(th) century. The slavs, who inhabited a large part of Eastern Europe, and were white, were taken as slaves by Spanish Muslims during the 9^(th) century AD. The Greek word was *doulos,* and the Hebrew word was *ebed.* There were strict rules regarding the treatment of slaves in the Bible. Some slaves were captured, and some were purchased. However, someone could also willingly become a slave to pay off debt.

Of the *African* slaves, Spain and Portugal had the most, followed by England (although, if you add the Irish slaves, then England moves to the front. This is where I come from. Search irisheyesofva.com). Of all the slave owning countries, only Denmark had fewer than the United States. This does not make it right; it just puts it in a different perspective.

In 1807, the United States criminalized the importation of slaves. They were the first country in the world to do so, with England following suit a few weeks later. Many countries still permit slavery today. China, who we now support, is just one example. The fight to free slaves was led by Christians in the U.S. and abroad dating back to early colonial times.

One of the leaders of the abolition movement in England was an evangelical Anglican cleric named John Newton. Newton was a former captain of slave ships and an investor in the slave trade. He almost died in a storm at sea and became a Christian shortly after. Newton wrote the hymn *Amazing Grace* in 1772. In 1833, England abolished African slavery, followed by the U.S. in 1865 after the Civil War. England did not abolish the Irish slave trade until a bill was passed in 1839.

Much of Black history has been kept out of the history books in our schools.

Crispus Attucks, a free black man, was the first casualty in the American Revolution. He was killed in the Boston Massacre.

James Armistead Lafayette, a Black servant and American spy, served in British General Cornwallis' quarters. He relayed information to General Washington that led to the defeat of the British forces at Yorktown, which brought victory for the American forces in the war.

Lemuel Haynes was an American clergyman, the first Black American to be ordained as a minister and was a veteran of the American Revolution.

Free Christians of all colors banded together in faith to lead the charge to free all people.

Woodrow Wilson, the 28th president of the United States, wrote a history textbook that celebrated the Confederacy and, in particular, the Ku Klux Klan. He segregated the Federal government and rolled back many of the hard-fought economic victories for Black Americans. He supported the theory of evolution and claimed that being white was a more advanced stage of evolution, while being Black was closer to a neanderthal. *Really?* As stated earlier, *loss* of DNA brought white skin, light hair and eyes. The theory of evolution promotes inequality and racism.

I personally think that Yahweh uses all things (even the bad) to point us to Him. We never would have had the opportunity to have heard the words, witnessed the true bravery, seen the accomplishments, or been exposed to such great, thought-provoking leaders such as Dr. Martin Luther King Jr., Rosa Parks, Katherine Johnson, Duke Ellington, George Washington Carver, and Thomas Sowell. According to a 2007 Pew Research survey, 87% of African Americans identify as

Christian compared to 83% of the rest of America. 79% of African Americans state that "religion is very important in their life," compared to 56% of the rest of us.

The Bible is the Word of God. It says that all are equal in the eyes of our Father, and we are to love all His creation. We are equal in our sins, and we are equal in our need for a Savior, Jesus Christ.

The truth, while not popular with the secular world, is nonetheless so much healthier and more interesting for our souls.

Humans have a long way to go to be righteous. We cannot do it alone. We *must* accept Jesus Christ as our Lord and Savior. We must love and respect each other and obey the Law found in His Word. We must study actual history and learn from it. We cannot let the mainstream news teach us their doctrine, (search If I Were The Devil, by Paul Harvey, 1965 on YouTube), **We are moving backward!** The so-called experts waffle from one idea to another trying to cover up the lies that are causing division and separating us from our Father and our Savior. What happened in Venezuela is now happening in Israel, the United States, and around the world.

"For the wrath of God is revealed from heaven against all ungodliness and unrighteousness of men, who suppress the truth in unrighteousness, because what may be known of God is manifest in them, for God has shown it to them. For since the creation of the world His invisible attributes are clearly seen, being understood by the things that are made, even His eternal power and Godhead, so that they are without excuse, because, although they knew God, they did not glorify Him as God, nor were thankful, but became futile in their thoughts, and their foolish hearts were darkened. Professing to be wise, they became fools, and changed the glory of the incorruptible God into an image made like corruptible man—and birds and four-footed animals and creeping things.

"Therefore God also gave them up to uncleanness, in the lusts of their hearts, to dishonor their bodies among themselves, who exchanged the truth of God for the lie, and worshiped and served the creature rather than the Creator, who is blessed forever. Amen" (Romans 1:18-25).

Jesus was not born into affluence. Yahweh saw to it that He was born into the lowest of positions. Two teenagers found themselves in a particularly precarious position. Mary was betrothed to Joseph and became pregnant. This would have been an offense worthy of stoning at the time. Joseph was planning to quietly divorce her until an angel spoke to him in a dream. Only the head of household needed to show up to be counted during the census, yet Joseph took Mary with him to Bethlehem. Maybe to keep her safe from the townspeople? Regardless of the reason, this fulfilled the prophecy about the Messiah's birth. His birth was witnessed by animals. Angels announced the birth to shepherds (who were lumped in with the sinners according to society). The baby was visited by Gentile Magi from the east (c.f., the Chaldeans in the Book of Daniel. The Magi had been taught by Daniel and were watching for the star). This was not the auspicious beginning for a King expected by modern standards, but it was a perfect beginning by Yahweh's standards. Jesus was the perfect example of humility. He came to save and serve sinners—the people who need Him the most and who can relate to Him the easiest.

Christians worship a God who pursues them instead of needing to be pursued by them.

"He who believes in Me, believes not in Me but in Him who sent Me. And he who sees Me sees Him who sent Me. I have come as a light into the world, that whoever believes in Me should not abide in darkness. And if anyone hears My words and does not believe, I do not judge him; for I did not come to judge the world but to

save the world. He who rejects Me, and does not receive My words, has that which judges him—the word that I have spoken will judge him in the last day. For I have not spoken on My own authority; but the Father who sent Me gave Me a command, what I should say and what I should speak. And I know that His command, is everlasting life. Therefore, whatever I speak, just as the Father has told Me, so I speak" (John 12:44-50).

Jesus came to serve us and to save us. He taught us what it means to follow Yahweh in humility. He taught love and self-sacrifice. Jesus left His place in a perfect Heaven to come to this sin-filled, self-centered, little orb in the vast universe of His Fathers creation for *our benefit*, not His. Jesus did not have to come for His sake, He had to come for *ours*. We have only to believe in His death and resurrection, that He came to save us, and that Yahweh will forgive us and grant us righteousness.

Sharing Yeshua with others is critical. The rapture of the church *will* happen. With millions of people gone from the world all at once, many that have heard, but not accepted the word, will come to faith in Yeshua. They will be the tribulation saints.

Father in Heaven, holy be Your name, Thy Kingdom come, Thy will be done on earth as it is in Heaven.

Please open the hearts and minds of Your children to Your Holy Spirit. Let their eyes see and their ears hear.

Forgive us of our sins and help us to forgive those who have sinned against us.

In the name of our Lord and Savior Jesus Christ, amen.

This prayer that follows was copied from the Billy Graham Evangelistic Association's website:

"Dear God, I know I'm a sinner, and I ask for Your forgiveness. I believe Jesus Christ is Your Son. I believe that He died for my sin and that You raised Him to life. I want to trust Him as my Savior and follow Him as Lord, from this day forward. Guide my life and help me to do Your will. I pray this in the name of Jesus. Amen."

Continue to
STAND
LOVE
SUPPORT
and
TEACH.
But above all,
STAND.

Acknowledgments

At the beginning, I stated some of the sources that I used in my study. Here, I will go a little further.

I owe all that I have learned to Jesus and to the Christian men and women whom I have had the privilege to learn from. Without their perseverance in teaching the Gospel and their love for all of Yahweh's creation, we would have no opportunity to know Jesus and His offer of salvation.

I am in a constant state of gratitude, humility, and awe of our Father, Yahweh; His son, Yeshua the Messiah; and His Holy Spirit. His pursuit of us for our salvation is constant and never-ending. The love displayed by our Creator for us is visible and deeply felt.

Thank you.

I also want to thank Grace Church in Overland Park, Kansas. Senior Pastor Tim Howey and Campus Pastor Justin Raby have created an atmosphere that welcomes all with love and understanding. This attitude permeates the entire church. Arriving at the campus brings an actual smile to my face. What I appreciate the most is the honest delivery of the truth, no matter whose feathers get ruffled. This church and the people who serve it started me down the path to salvation, and they continue to challenge and teach me.

Their website is visitgracechurch.com with links to YouTube, Facebook, Instagram, and Twitter.

These are the Christian authors whose words I have read and quoted:

Lee Strobel: *The Case for Christ* (and I have started reading *The Case for Miracles*). I will read both multiple times. He is a journalist who knows how to write so that even I can understand. He was an atheist who set out to disprove the Bible. He is no longer an atheist; now he is a Christian pastor and teacher.

Strobel says, "If your friend is sick and dying, the most important thing he wants is not an explanation; he wants you to sit with him. He's terrified of being alone more than anything else. So, God has not left us alone." (godtube.com)

J. Warner Wallace: *Person of Interest* and *Cold Case Christianity*. Wallace is a renowned cold-case investigator who has been featured on Dateline and other television shows for his detective work. He was also a non-believer until 1996 when he became a Christian after investigating Jesus. His books describe how he investigated and what that investigation revealed to him.

A quote from Wallace: "I am a Christian today for one reason: Christianity is true. I'm a Christian because I want to live in a way that reflects the truth, even if it's hard, inconvenient, or unpopular. I'm a Christian because my high regard for the truth leaves me no alternative. An inconvenient truth is preferable to a convenient lie." Cold Case Christianity Updated Version: A Homicide Detective Investigates the Claims of the Gospels.

Philip Yancey: *The Jesus I Never Knew*. Reading this book was when I first faced the fact that Jesus was Jewish. I knew this, but I never thought about it. You wouldn't think that it would matter, but to me it did. It put the "why" and "where" of Jesus in order.

Yancey said, "No one who meets Jesus ever stays the same. In the end I found the process of writing this book to be a great act of faith-strengthening. Jesus has rocked my own preconceptions and has made me ask the hard questions about why those of us who bear His name don't do a better job of following him." (The Jesus I Never Knew, Zondervan Publishing House).

There are a few Christian writers and teachers that I had originally wanted to include in this, however I discovered that they did not believe in the beginning. They support the idea of millions of years and of evolution. I could not, in good conscience, include them. We cannot blend the secular with the Biblical. It did not take an all-powerful Creator of the universe millions of years to get it right. It happened as stated in Genesis, in six days.

Internet Sources:

Gotquestions.org

Bibleref.com

Biblegateway.com

YouTube Channels:

Is Genesis History

Answers in Genesis

Expedition Bible.

These are just a smattering of the many sources available on the internet. These are the ones that piqued my interest, so I explored them. You should search out others; I do.

Christian radio:

I listen to Bott Radio, which broadcasts Christian news, commentary, and pastoral teaching 24/7. Bottradionetwork.com will allow you to search different stations near you.

Any Christian radio station will work, but Bott is available to me, so that is the one I listen to.

I mentioned earlier that investing in quality study materials is well worth the time and effort spent on your growth. I went on Amazon and searched for the highest-rated resources. Here is a list of what I invested in:

Strong's Complete and Exhaustive Concordance. This is the internet in book form. It's a must-have for when information is no longer available to us on the computer.

Nelson's Illustrated Bible Dictionary. It contains explanations that can be transferred to today's world.

Zondervan Atlas of the Bible. It is nice to follow the story on a map to gain a better understanding.

I have several study Bibles in different translations. I kind of went overboard, just a little. I did that because comparing the wording of the different translations is helpful for me to understand, but I also like to see that they all say the same thing. That's kind of a big deal. On a side note, any translation that replaces behemoth with hippopotamus in the Book of Job, I put it back on the shelf. Just my preference for the truth.

Honorable mentions:

Josh McDowell and his son Sean McDowell: *More Than a Carpenter* and *Evidence That Demands a Verdict*. I have just started reading these, and I love them. I heard of these books from other sources, which made me decide to purchase them.

C. S. Lewis. No list of Christian resources would be complete without mentioning Lewis. He has affected Christian Apologetics more than can be imagined.

These men (other than Sean McDowell) were atheists or non-believers who set out to prove the Bible wrong. Now, they are leaders in Christian Apologetics.

Lastly, to my God and my Savior, I give thanks for their love and for bringing into my life the many people who have led me down the narrow path to my Lord, Jesus.

Psalm 2

Why do the nations conspire
    and the peoples plot in vain?
The kings of the earth rise up
and the rulers band together
against the Lord
and against his anointed, saying,
"Let us break their chains
and throw off their shackles."
The One enthroned in heaven
laughs;
the Lord scoffs at them.
He rebukes them in his anger
and terrifies them in his wrath,
saying,
"I have installed my king
on Zion, my holy mountain."
I will proclaim the Lord's decree:
He said to me, "You are my son;
today I have become your father.
Ask of me,
and I will make the nations your
inheritance,
the ends of the earth your
possession.
You will break them with a rod of iron;

you will dash them to pieces like
pottery."
Therefore, you kings, be wise;
be warned, you rulers of the earth.
Serve the Lord with fear
and celebrate his rule with trembling.
Kiss his son, or he will be angry
and your way will lead to destruction,
for his wrath can flare up in a
moment.
Blessed are all who take refuge in
Him.

In Heaven, there will be no pain, no suffering. Yahweh has promised to wipe away all of our tears. I wonder who will wipe away His tears from all of the pain that we have caused Him.

Stand firm on the promise of our Father Yahweh and on the salvation offered by our Lord and Savior, Yeshua the Messiah.

Also by LeRoy Dunn

Jehovah Shalom The Lord is Peace
In Pursuit Of Us

About the Author

Ex-Naval Special Warfare, ex-truck driver, current HVAC technician. During a very eventful life, spent thinking that I was a good person and would be going to heaven, I found out, not so much.

I fortunately found Jesus and was saved.

Please join me in searching for salvation through Jesus Christ.